# BRISTOL CINEMAS

# BRISTOL CINEMAS

DAVE STEPHENSON AND JILL WILLMOTT

*Frontispiece*: The Bedminster Hippodrome.

First published 2005

Tempus Publishing Limited
The Mill, Brimscombe Port,
Stroud, Gloucestershire, GL5 2QG
www.tempus-publishing.com

© Dave Stephenson and Jill Willmott, 2005

British Library Cataloguing in Publication Data.
A catalogue record for this book is available from the British Library.

ISBN 0 7524 3669 4

Typesetting and origination by Tempus Publishing Limited.
Printed in Great Britain.

# CONTENTS

# ACKNOWLEDGEMENTS

Much of the history of Bristol cinemas has come from Bristol newspapers of the last 100 years, and we have credited where possible all those people who wrote for and to those newspapers. We would like to thank Gerry Brooke of the *Bristol Evening Post*, who allowed access to their archives.

We are grateful to Bristol Central Library and Bristol Record Office. Special thanks go to former cinema owner Denys Chamberlain and former projectionist Wally Ball, who must also be considered cinema historians.

Thanks also to (in no particular order) the late David Harrison, Jean Stone, John Duggan, Elsie Pyke, Stan Nash, John M. East, J. Coe, Dave Cheesley, Andy Jones, Jean Hobbs, Evelyn Parfitt (*née* Palmer), Brian Hodges, Joe Diorazio, Jean Sylvester, Roy Pugsley, Mrs D. Pugsley, Mary Glass, Beryl Farrall, Steve James, Chris and Rita Garland, Don and Stella Payne, Janet and Derek Fisher, A. Dring, Bryan Haynes, John Penny, John Bartlett, Collette Lovell, Sydney Gamlin, Jim McNeill, Mike Baker, Mike Hooper, Jonathan Rowe, Bill Knight, Frank Jenkins, R.C. Wyatt, David Foot, Jack Phelps, Anton Bantock, Mr A. Bayly, Mary Gazzard, Mr Athersuch, Reg Howlett, John Gould, Dennis Stephenson, Les Stephenson, John Boalch, Ray Miller, J. Fowler, Anna Miles, Patricia Edmead, Mrs L. Davies, Mr S.E. Smith, Brislington Conservation and History Society, Audrey Phillips, Edward Taylor, Mr Langford, Mr Gerrish, Cynthia Otley, Babs Lewis, George and Gary White, and Fishponds Library.

It is the intention of the authors to produce a second book about Bristol cinemas, which will hopefully cover more about the people who worked in, or were involved in some way with, the city's cinemas. If you have any pictures or information that may help us or if you have any comments regarding this book, please contact:

Dave Stephenson
7 New Cheltenham Road
Kingswood
Bristol
BS15 1TH

# SELECT BIBLIOGRAPHY

Anderson, Charles, *A City and its Cinemas*, Redcliffe Press Ltd, 1983
Bye, Maurice, *Castle Park Before the Blitz*, Tempus Publishing Ltd, 2003
Bristol Writers, *Dream On*, New Words, 1982
Foot, David, *Hungry Fighters of the West*, Redcliffe Press
Hallett, Terry, *Bristols Forgotten Empire*, Badger Press, 2000
Robinson, Christopher, *The History of Bristol Hippodrome*, Prosceniun, 1982

# ꟼNTRODUCTION

The first films to be seen by a Bristol audience were brought to the city by travelling showmen, who often hired local halls such as Kingsley Hall in Old Market. John M. East recalls that, many years ago, his great-uncle John Codman started out hiring halls and then bought a portable cinema. When in Bristol, he would park up on one of the local commons, such as Horfield, and shout 'Walk up! See my stupendous attraction! See people come alive in pictures!' His mobile cinema was hauled by a traction engine which also served to generate power to operate the projector and light a canvas screen. It could easily hold 600 people and even had a £1,000 Chiappi organ, which Codman used to attract his audience and also to drown out his rivals. He made his own films, both comic and dramatic. Bill-posting and publicity preceded his arrival in town, and on the day before the show opened he would tour the main streets, standing on the back of an open lorry. A camera would be fixed to the floor, with an assistant vigorously turning the handle. Codman would shout from the lorry, 'Come and see yourselves on the screen! A handsome prize for those who can recognise themselves.' Only a few minutes of film was shot but the people flocked in to see it. Codman made lots of money and the audience saw what they thought was magical.

As film became more popular, buildings that had previously had other uses – such as dance halls, theatres and even ice rinks – were converted into cinemas. To protect the public, fire regulations were introduced by an Act of Parliament in 1910. These converted buildings became known as penny gaffs. Four of them appeared in Bristol around 1909: the Bio, the Vestry, the Gem and Bedminster Town Hall. By the 1920s, there were about thirty-five scattered around Bristol. In the early days, most had rows of wooden benches, sometimes nailed to the floor to stop them being stolen, and a single projector standing in the gangway.

From these humble beginnings came the purpose-built cinemas, the first being the Queen's Picture House. Others quickly followed. The cinemas were frequented mainly by the working class; the upper classes called them 'the poor man's theatre'. In March 1929, the 'talkies' arrived at the King's cinema in Old Market. The film was *The Singing Fool* with Al Jolson. All of the Bristol cinemas were wired for sound by the middle of 1931. This meant that orchestras and pianists were no longer needed and they lost their jobs overnight. A few were kept on to play in the interval and some became managers.

In the 1930s, new Hollywood-style cinemas based on classical design started to appear in Bristol, with bigger auditoriums, large foyers, cafés and restaurants. They even used floodlights inside and out, to highlight the building. At least fifteen new picture houses were built at this time, the biggest being the Odeon in Broadmead and the Embassy in Queens Avenue. Most of the smaller cinemas had to modernise just to stay in business. Three giant cinema groups emerged at this time: the Gaumont, Odeon and ABC Group networks soon covered the whole country. These large cinema chains were tied to major film companies like MGM, 20th Century Fox, First National and Universal, which gave them first choice on the best films.

In 1932, the Sunday Entertainment Act stopped cinemas opening on Sundays.

However, during the Second World War the government decided to reopen cinemas after an initial trial closure and allowed Sunday opening. It was thought that people needed entertainment and a morale booster, and they could also watch newsreels. Bristol suffered badly during the war, and two of the city's best cinemas – the Regent in Castle Street and the Triangle in Clifton – were lost in late 1940, when the heart of Bristol was bombed. If the Sunday opening ban had been lifted a week earlier, the cinemas would have been full and the casualties very high. The Redcliffe, the Avonmouth and the Stoll in Bedminster were also destroyed during the war.

After the Second World War, many people moved out of the city to new housing estates. Television became more popular, with many people buying a set to watch the Coronation in 1953. Between 1945 and 1965, seventeen of Bristol's cinemas closed and no new ones opened. In 1947, the city council debated Sunday opening, which led to a public vote. It was won with a majority of 5, 804, but only 17 per cent of the public had bothered to vote.

Film makers tried to win back audiences, producing films such as *The Robe* in Cinemascope and *White Christmas* in VistaVision. They also tried to attract people with films that featured permissiveness, juvenile delinquency and racial intolerance but, as Sam Goldwyn of MGM said at the time, 'Why should people go out and pay money to see bad films when they can stay at home and watch bad television for nothing!'

The larger cinema companies had the monopoly on the big films, which were then passed to their smaller branches. Smaller cinemas needed investment but didn't often get it. The cinema became the haunt of courting couples, who didn't care what film was showing. Teddy Boys wrecked the seats and nobody really noticed how shabby the buildings were. These once-proud picture houses became known as fleapits.

One by one the cinemas closed. They became supermarkets, hardware stores, pubs and even churches. Many became bingo halls – the latest craze. Many were demolished. By the mid-1960s, only a handful were still open. Saturday morning showings were still popular, especially at the ABC cinema where they had their own Minors' Club. In the late 1960s and early 1970s, film clubs and studios opened up and by the 1980s the new breed of supercinema was opening at out-of-town developments. The days of the privately owned cinemas had gone.

Dave Stephenson and Jill Willmott
*June 2005*

# A–Z OF BRISTOL CINEMAS

## ABC, New Bristol Centre, Frogmore Street, 1966-1997

The ABC opened in 1966; it was the first new cinema in Bristol for over twenty-five years and became the flagship for ABC in Bristol. All the top films were shown there and were then passed to the smaller ABC venues.

Eighteenth-century houses had been demolished for this very bland building. Its sheer size dwarfed everything around it. Designed by Gillison, Barnett and Partner, it opened as an entertainment complex which included a cinema, dance hall, ice rink, nightclub and bingo hall. The cinema had a single screen and seating for 800 people in the stalls and the balcony. It is remembered for its long curtains which parted to reveal a gently curving screen with a spectacular sound system. The foyer and lounge bar were very modern and the cinema claimed to be 'the best in the west!'.

The ABC was opened by the Lord Mayor with trumpet fanfares. The first film shown was *Dr Zhivago*. It became a two-screen cinema in 1980 and closed in October 1997. In the following year, part of the complex was demolished to make way for flats and the old cinema was turned into the Rock nightclub (now the Carling Academy). The famous Hatchet Inn stands opposite.

*The ABC in the New Bristol Centre, c. 1987.*

*The Bedminster Odeon during its time as the Top Rank Club.*

# Ambassador/Odeon, Winterstoke Road, Bedminster, 1936-1961

The old Bedminster Odeon, situated at the junction of Winterstoke Road and Luckwell Road, started life as the Ambassador in 1936. With its striking round tower, it has been described as looking like a cathedral. It had a red neon sign running down its white exterior and seated 1,250 on a single sloping floor. The Odeon group, which had merged with Gaumont British under the control of J. Arthur Rank, took over the cinema, along with the Kingswood branch, just after the Second World War. The Odeon in Broadmead and the Gaumont in Baldwin Street got the big films first and then they were sent to the two smaller branches. This worked well until bingo became more profitable. The Odeon closed in 1961 and was the Top Rank Club in the 1970s. The building has now been renovated and is a children's play centre called the Alphabet Zoo.

*The interior of the Ambassador, Kingswood, which was later renamed the Odeon.*

# Ambassador/Odeon, Kingswood, 1938-1961

Opened by Captain Sir D.W. Gunstan on 26 March 1938, the Ambassador's first manager was F. Hozier. The art deco building had a red and blue neon light on its tower and a stained-glass window in the stairway commemorating local hero W.G. Grace. There was a very smart café above the foyer. The cinema had a huge balcony and could seat almost 2,000 in its comfortable dark blue seats.

During the Blitz in 1940, the Ambassador lost its roof when a mine exploded at the rear of the building. Fortunately, no one was seriously hurt, although a salesgirl was blown out of the cinema and into the foyer.

When Oscar Deutsch took over after the Second World War, the Ambassador was renamed the Odeon and redecorated in red and gold. It closed on 11 March 1961, having been bought by Rank. It was converted into a ten-pin bowling alley.

# Ashton/Plaza, No. 275 North Street, Bedminster, 1914-1954

The Ashton stood at the junction of North Street and Raleigh Road. S.F. Harris was recorded as the owner until the late 1930s, when A.B. Atkinson took over. At this time, Mr Atkinson also owned the nearby Redcliffe and Bedminster Town Hall. The Ashton was a very small, family-friendly cinema. It was very well kept and in the late 1920s seats were often booked in advance, mainly by young couples.

After the film and newsreel had finished, the film boy had to jump on his bike and take it to the Redcliffe or the Town Hall, hoping it wasn't raining. The cinema had no orchestra, just a single piano. In later years, it was called the Plaza but it was too small to survive, as the nearby Rex and Odeon were more attractive to customers. It closed in 1954 and was converted into a supermarket. It later became a furniture showroom, as it still is today. Upstairs, in what is now the offices, you can still see the ornate cinema ceiling. Outside, the stone inscribed '1914' can still be seen.

*The Plaza, formerly the Ashton.*

*Today (2005), the building is a shop selling carpets and beds.*

# Avonmouth (Portview), Portview Road, 1912-1940

Built in 1912 for the new shipping centre at Avonmouth, this cinema replaced a steam laundry at the end of a row of buildings in Portview Road, between Collins Street and Farr Street. It had a triangular interior and the screen was off-centre, causing strained necks for those sitting on the right. It was called the Avonmouth but was known locally as the Portview because it was in Portview Road.

The cinema was bombed in the Blitz of 1940; its last owner was W.J. Rolph. Soon after the air raid, Roy Chamberlain, owner of the Gaiety, the Knowle and the Broadway, was in Avonmouth with his son Denys. Rolph allowed Denys to take the old projector from the bombed cinema home. He worked on it and, with the aid of an old vacuum cleaner motor, got it going again.

# Baths Cinema, Gloucester Road, Bishopston, 1922-1936

The old Bristol North Baths were often empty in winter, when no one wanted to swim, and so they were converted into the Baths cinema, which opened on 1 August 1922. The pool had been drained and a wooden floor, which took a week to lay, had been placed over the tiled area. The cinema had hard seats at the front and padded seats at the back; the three-sided viewing area above the pool served as a balcony. In the summer months, the cinema was turned back into a swimming pool. Bruce Atkinson was the first person to lease this building from the city council. Atkinson was also involved at Zetland Road, the Dolphin, the Vestry, the Redcliffe, Bedminster Town Hall, the Plaza, the Scala, the Kingsway and the Regent at Kingswood. In 1936, the Baths once more became a swimming pool all year round.

*A 2005 photograph of Bristol North Baths, which was employed as the Baths cinema until 1936.*

# Bio Pictureland, The Counterslip, Bath Street, 1908-1918

The Bio Pictureland, or the Bio, as it was always known, was Bristol's first permanent cinema, set up in the existing Counterslip Hall. In its early days, the Bio was advertised as the 'Cinematograph Show Specialist'. It was owned by Frank W. Ogden Smith, who opened his first cinema in Clapham in 1907 and by 1910 had eight dotted around the south of the country. The cinema seated 600 people on long, hard and uncomfortable benches on a single floor. Tickets cost a penny to sit at the front and twopence at the back and you could get a cup of tea after the afternoon show. The doorman was described by some as 'an evil-looking bloke with one eye'; he wore a second-hand postman's uniform, including a cap with its Post Office badge torn off. The Bio was eventually demolished and the old Courage's building now stands on the site.

# Brislington Picture Hall, Sandy Park Road, 1913-1956

This was one of the earliest cinemas in this part of Bristol. It was situated on the junction of Sandy Park Road and Belmont Road and was at first called the Empress but this was short-lived. The cinema was owned by the Tomkins family, who also had another business, Bristol Film Services Ltd, at No. 127 Victoria Street. They supplied silent films to local cinemas; the music was supplied by a piano, with an occasional violin or accordion. In 1938, it was announced that the Ritz cinema was to be built at the junction of Bristol Hill and Warrington Road. The Tomkins family made many objections but to no avail. They were eventually forced to carry out major renovations to try and compete with the bigger and more modern cinema. The Brislington Picture Hall survived until December 1956. By now, George Tomkins had taken over from his father but television and poor films had taken their toll on what was now known just as the Brislington cinema. It remained closed for several years, reopening as the Brislington Bingo Hall in 1962. This was owned by the Chamberlain family, who also owned several Bristol cinemas. (*see* the Magnet, the Gaiety, the Knowle and the Broadway). Today, the Brislington Picture Hall has been converted into flats with the rather nice name of Kinema House, owned by the United Housing Association.

*Brislington Picture Hall.*

# Bristol Hippodrome, No. 13 St Augustine's Parade, 1932-1938

In 1911, Mr Oswald Stoll applied for a licence to build a music hall and cinematography exhibition at No. 13 St Augustine's Parade. At that time, the council considered the site to be residential property of an undesirable class, so were in favour of any improvement. There was some opposition, as there were already several music halls in the area, but Mr Stoll got his licence, promising 'high-class theatre' as opposed to 'rough music hall'. The theatre opened on Monday 16 December 1912 and some of the great stars of the day appeared on its stage. Cary Grant was an apprentice there for a short time. For a period of two weeks in September 1929, a full-length 'talkie' film was shown. *This is Heaven* starred Vilma Dalky and James Hal and was so popular that it was decided that the Hippodrome would become a full-time cinema. Live theatre ended in October 1932 and the band played out with 'Auld Lang Syne'. The management hoped the change of use to a cinema would be only temporary; they were right. The first film shown was *Congorilla*, a film shot entirely in Africa, but already people were asking why such a beautiful theatre was being wasted on films. After just six years, it closed for renovation and alteration before being reopened as a theatre. Films were shown there in June and July 1939 but that was the last time. Since then, the Hippodrome has been Bristol's premier theatre.

*Two pages from a 1930s copy of* The Stoll Herald, *which advertised forthcoming films at the Bristol Hippodrome.*

# Broadway, Filwood Park, 1938-1961

This cinema was part of a plan to build a mini-estate complete with houses, shops, a swimming pool, a library and a petrol station, with the main road running nearby for easy access. Within a ½ mile radius of the site of Filwood Broadway, 3,100 houses were proposed, with a further 450 within two years. Within a ½ mile radius of Leinster Avenue, 1,600 houses were proposed, with a further 750 within two years. Therefore the area would be in need of the proposed facilities. The licence to build the cinema was put out to tender in 1937. It was won by Roy Chamberlain (*see* the Gaiety/Knowle) but there were conditions. The cinema had to have a frontage of 62ft and a depth of 112ft. It was to cost not less than £13,000 and be completed within fifteen months. The council loaned Chamberlain £7,000 in the form of a mortgage at an interest rate of 4 per cent. The lease was for ninety-nine years and would be charged at £22 per annum for the first seven years, rising to £34 after fourteen years. The council also put in a clause stating that a door at the rear of the cinema, with its own pay box, was 'desirable to enable the lower class of patrons to use the back entrance'.

The cinema opened on 20 October 1938. The opening ceremony was performed by Alderman Charles Gill, the chairman of the housing committee, who later became Lord Mayor. After the film show, people were asked to remain in their seats for light refreshments. The cinema seated 1,160 people and was built by local firm R.J. Hurford, with Dennis Hurford and Roy Chamberlain acting as architects. It had a saucer-shaped ground floor instead of the usual rake or tiers, which gave the audience a good view of the screen wherever they were sitting. Walter Luckes was the first manager, followed by E.E. Jones and Fred Godwin. Once when a child had forgotten his entrance money for the matinee, one of these managers allowed him in to see the film, on the understanding that he brought the money the following week. By the next week, word had gone round and there were two queues outside: one of children who had their money and the other queue of children who had forgotten theirs!

The Broadway did not just show films. Bingo started there in August 1961, on Saturday nights only, and soon became very popular. There was even a national link which paid out large sums of money and there were visits from celebrities, including Stan Stennet and Bristol Rovers manager Bert Tann. At one big bingo game they closed the doors early, leaving lots of local regulars outside. The regulars threatened to lynch Denys Chamberlain (who had taken over the cinema from his father) and he had to be smuggled out of the building by a back door. Thursday was boxing night at the Broadway. A series of boxing matches was organised by Len Munden, a former boxer who lost an arm and went on to become the only one-armed PSV bus driver in the country. The cinema was also used as a concert venue. The Eagles, a famous Bristol group, played there; they later featured in the Bristol film *Some People*, which starred Kenneth Moore. The biggest concert held there was by P.J. Proby in July 1964. A few girls fainted as he sang hits like 'I Believe' and 'Hold Me', often drowned out by the screaming fans.

Denys Chamberlain sold the Broadway in the late 1980s and it closed a few years later. Its old Kalee 12 projectors and many of its chairs are stored in Bristol's Industrial Museum. Locals have tried to get one of the supermarket chains to take over the building but it is now hoped that the Knowle West Development Trust might do so instead.

Opposite: *The Bristol Hippodrome, c. 1920.*

*The Broadway under construction, c. 1938.*

*Mr & Mrs F. G. W. Chamberlain*

*request the pleasure of the Company of*

*at the Opening of*

*The Broadway Cinema,*

*Filwood Park, Knowle,*

*On Thursday, October 20th, 1938, at 7 p.m.*

**WILL YOU PLEASE RETURN THE ENCLOSED CARD, DULY FILLED IN, BEFORE OCTOBER 17TH, 1938.**

**AFTER THE PERFORMANCE PLEASE RETAIN YOUR SEATS, WHEN LIGHT REFRESHMENTS WILL BE SERVED**

*An invitation to the opening ceremony at the Broadway on 20 October 1938.*

# BOXING

LEN MUNDEN'S PROMOTIONS

## THURSDAY, 19th FEBRUARY, 1970

DOORS OPEN 7 pm    START 7.30 pm

## BROADWAY CINEMA

KNOWLE — BRISTOL

---

8 x 3  Sensational Light-Heavy Weight Contest at 12-st 9-lbs

## ALAN BALL v. DERVIN AIREY

| BARGOED | BRISTOL |
|---|---|
| 1968 ABA Champion | MacWilliam Stable. Recently top of |
| One of Eddie Thomas's Boys | the bill Anglo American Sporting Club. |

A FUTURE CHAMPION HERE ? ?

---

6 x 3  Smashing Middle Weight Contest at 11-st. 8-lbs.

## RAY HASSAN v. CLIVE COOK

| ST. HELENS | CARDIFF |
|---|---|
| One of Peter Fletcher's boys | Topped Bill with Len Gibs at N.S.C. in December |

A RETURN CONTEST

---

6 x 3  Brilliant Feather Weight Contest at 9-st. 3-lbs.

## BOBBY FISHER v. SELECTED OPPONENT

| BRISTOL | Watch Local Press |
|---|---|
| Needs No Introduction | |

---

6 x 3  All Action Light Heavy Weight Contest at 12-st. 9-lbs.

## PATRICK MAHONEY v. FRED DRINAN

| CARDIFF | GLOUCESTER |
|---|---|
| Fighting Irish Man | Now Fit and Well |

---

Plus — ANOTHER 6 Rd. CONTEST

---

Reserved Seats : £2–0–0 Ground Floor (Ringside)
Remainder of Ground Floor : £1–0–0 & 10/–
Reserved Seats : £1–0–0 Balcony 1st & 2nd Rows
Remainder of Balcony : 10/– & 5/–

Ticket enquiries : Bristol 76145 and Broadway Cinema 663336

Your support will be Greatly Appreciated. Come along and help to put Bristol back in its rightful place in the BOXING WORLD

ALL BOXERS ARE LICENSED UNDER THE BRITISH BOXING BOARD OF CONTROL CONTRACT TO APPEAR AT THE ABOVE HALL — LEN MUNDEN

---

G. & M. Organ, Wrington, Bristol.

*Boxing at the Broadway was a popular event.*

Above: *P.J. Proby at the Broadway, July 1964.*

Right: *An advertisement for films showing at local cinemas, including* Q Planes *at the Broadway.*

Below: *The Broadway, 2005.*

# Cabot, Filton, 1935–1961

The Cabot, a striking building at the junction of Braemar Avenue and Gloucester Road North, opened on Monday 7 October 1935. The first film shown was a new British film, *Drake of England* (known in America as *Drake the Pirate*), which starred Matheson Lang, Athene Seyler and Jane Baxter. The cinema was built by Sidney Gamlin, who bought the Park cinema and also built the Vandyck. The Cabot was designed by W.H. Watkins and seated 1,114 people. Mr Gamlin leased it to the ABC chain almost from the start. When the Shirley Temple film *Bright Eyes*, featuring the song 'On the Good Ship Lollipop', was shown at the Cabot, the children were given free lollipops. This made it a memorable day for the children and, with lollipops costing next to nothing, it was cheap advertising for the cinema.

From May 1939, the cinema was used as a recruitment centre for the ARP services, auxiliary firemen, air-raid wardens, decontamination and rescue units, and first-aid personnel. Filton was, of course, a prime target during the Second World War because of its aircraft factories.

In 1956, Sidney Gamlin took the cinema back from ABC when the lease ran out. Falling attendances, due to the popularity of television and the lack of good films, sealed its fate and it closed in July 1961. The staff had hoped for a good film to finish but instead a live rock and roll concert was staged and brought in the largest audience for years. After the cinema closed, many of the fixtures were sold to other cinemas around the country in a private sale. The pay box ended up at the Gaiety in Knowle. The building then became a Fine Fare supermarket, which opened in May 1962 with the Dagenham Girl Pipers and television personality Maureen Stafford in attendance. It later became a Blockbuster video store before being demolished to make way for flats.

*A view of the Cabot, showing the nearby shops.*

*The Cabot by day...*

*...and by night.*

*The Carlton.*

## Carlton, Canford Lane, Westbury-on-Trym, 1933-1959

Situated between Nos 11 and 19 Canford Lane, the Carlton was owned by George Allen, who also owned His Majesty's, Eastville Hippodrome and the early Metropole along with the Ritz at Brislington. This was one of W.H. Watkins' later designs, which was quite striking in its day but provided no shelter for the queuing public if it rained. It opened in 1933 with good bus routes from nearby Sea Mills, Henleaze, Henbury and Southmead and a bus stop right outside. It could seat 820. The Carlton closed in 1959, its last film being *The Reluctant Debutante*, starring Rex Harrison and Kay Kendall. The building was bought by a Cardiff-based company and demolished. The Carlton Court shopping precinct, named in honour of the cinema, was built in its place.

*An advertisement for Gunga Din and Risky Business at the Carlton.*

**THE CARLTON**
CINEMA, WESTBURY-ON-TRYM.
TO-DAY — — — Continuous from 1.45.
DOUGLAS FAIRBANKS, Jun , in
**"GUNGA DIN"**
(U)     At  2 14  -  5 30  --   8 45.
Also GEORGE MURPHY in
**"RISKY BUSINESS"**
(U)     At 4 5 and 7 20

# Cheltenham/Plaza/Academy, Cheltenham Road, 1914-1955

Most people remember this cinema as the Plaza or the Academy but it was originally called the Cheltenham. It was owned by Ralph Pringle, whose other cinema, the Zetland (later the Scala), was just along the road. Pringle called his company Cheltenham and Zetland Hall Ltd. In 1933, the cinema was sold to Emmanuel Harris and renamed the Plaza. Some time after 1940, Bruce Atkinson took over the Plaza. This means that over the years the cinema was owned by three of the greatest names in Bristol cinema – Pringle, Harris and Atkinson.

In the early 1950s, the cinema's name was changed again, this time to the Academy. It closed in 1955 and was purchased by the Christadelphians for £7,000, to be used as a place of worship. In 1998, Wetherspoon's opened it as a pub, spending £1 million on converting this old cinema into a modern drinking and eating establishment. It was given the inspired name of the Magic Box, in honour of William Frieze Greene.

The building, which is faced with red brick and has limestone dressing, is one of W.H. Watkins' best designs and is now Grade II listed.

*The Cheltenham.*

*The cinema became a Christadelphian Hall…*

*…and is now the Magic Box public house.*

# Cinema Picture Hall/Castle Street Cinema, No. 65 Castle Street, 1911-1926

Known as the Castle Street cinema, the Cinema Picture Hall opened in 1911 but lasted only fifteen years. It is thought that the building was formerly a sewing machine depot. This small picture house, which somehow managed to fit in a band, was an awkward place to find, as the entrance was in an alleyway. One of the early managers was Alexander Grant. In the afternoon you could buy a cup of tea and biscuits there and do some shopping in Castle Street, one of Bristol's prime shopping areas. The picture house closed in 1926, when Woolworths extended their premises.

# Clare Street Picture House, 1911-1927

The Clare Street Picture House was one of the cinemas that Cary Grant recalled visiting as a child. The official name of the cinema was the Picture House at Nos 9-11 Clare Street. It was wedged so tightly between Clare Street and Colston Avenue that its patrons entered from one street and went out on the other. Jean Stone recalls that:

> its interiors were covered in tapestries of eighteenth-century ladies on floral swings beneath the trees. The foyer with its dim lighting and soft carpets led either downstairs to the Oake Café or upstairs to the rosy glow of the Wedgewood Room, with its little sandwiches, three-tiered cake stands and dainty slices of bread and butter. The waitresses wore light grey with white muslin aprons and headbands. The walls matched, with grey surfaces and white garlands. The waitresses would also bring a tray of tea and cakes to your seat during the interlude.

The 470-seat cinema, which was built and owned by the Provincial Cinematograph Theatre Ltd, opened in July 1911. The Lord Mayor headed the speakers at the opening. The *Western Daily Press* said at the time that the cinema 'was constructed so that women need not remove their hats'. There were little lights to guide you to your seat and also page boys to take your hats and coats on entry. Employed at the cinema were five men and five women, with a Mrs O'Halloran in charge. Uniforms were inspected every day and hands and nails had to be clean and shoes polished. The men wore uniforms that were gold-braided with rows of buttons down the front of a short jacket.

In the end, the picture house was considered too small to survive and its owners built the Regent in Castle Street. The Clare Street Picture House closed in March 1927; the Regent opened in July 1928.

Opposite: *Clare Street Picture House in the 1920s.*

# Clifton Spa, 1920-1921

This cinema was situated next to the Avon Gorge Hotel but only survived for about a year, as it had problems obtaining a licence.

# Coliseum, Park Row, 1912-1924

Situated on the corner of Park Row and Woodland Road, this wedge-shaped building opened as a cinema in August 1912. It had previously been a roller-skating rink, an ice rink, an exhibition hall, a dance hall and even a car showroom, and almost didn't get its licence due to its constant change of use. During the First World War, it was used as an aircraft factory. Parnall & Sons made seaplanes for the Admiralty and aero-biplanes were assembled there.

The Coliseum had one floor and just 450 seats. At least three of the big names in Bristol cinema tried to make it pay – Ralph Bromhead, Emmanuel Harris and Roy Chamberlain each took their turn. They even hired a ladies' orchestra as a novelty to attract audiences. However, the cinema couldn't pay its way and closed in 1924.

The building was blitzed on 24 November 1940 and little was left but the exterior walls. It was temporarily re-roofed and used by the university, who now own it. It was later restored and in recent times a memorial to Nipper, the dog who featured in the HMV adverts, whose owner lived on the opposite side of the road, has been erected on the side of the building.

*The Coliseum.*

# Dolphin Picture House, Dolphin Street, 1910-1922

The Dolphin Picture House took its name from the street in which it was situated, which in turn took its name from the Dolphin Inn that once stood there. The street's previous name was Defence Lane. Narrow Wine Street used to lead from Dolphin Street to Castle Mill Street and Castle Green; much of this disappeared when Fairfax House was built.

The Dolphin, also known as the Kosy Korner Kinema, opened on 21 December 1910. It was owned by Ralph Pringle, who also built or leased the Pringle Palace (Scala), the Vestry and Bedminster Town Hall. The Dolphin was converted from two existing buildings, which were given a new frontage. The cinema seated just 500 people and consisted of a lobby and auditorium. It was considered quite a modest building, its only real feature being the screen edged in blue velvet.

In 1919, C. Parminton Cardell was the owner; later, Bruce Atkinson took over. The Dolphin probably would have survived for longer than its twelve years had it not been for a fire which started in the rewind room one Saturday night. This was a common occurrence in those days. The fire spread through the building and the cinema never reopened.

# Embassy, Queens Avenue, 1933-1963

When the Embassy was built in 1933, it was Bristol's biggest cinema. It was designed in collaboration with W.H. Watkins. Five other Bristol cinemas opened in that same year – the Cabot, the Carlton, the Gaiety, the News Theatre and the Savoy – and all except the Gaiety were designed by Watkins.

The Embassy's 170ft frontage dwarfed the surrounding buildings. An impressive neon display highlighted it at night. Inside were 2,000 lamps to highlight the ornamental ceiling, the velour wall drapes and the horizontally fluted columns that flanked the stage. It took a whole year to build, with 200 workmen on the site. It had a staff of 50 and there was a cinema cat, named Mitzi after the film star Mitzi Gaynor. The Embassy seated 2,100 people, including 700 in a spacious balcony, and could rightly be called 'the best in Bristol'. Stan Nash, a projectionist who had worked in many Bristol cinemas, said, 'Looking through the portals, it was like looking at a postage stamp! The screen was so far away'.

Concerts were held at the Embassy, usually on a Sunday evening. People like Joe Loss and Billy Cotton and their orchestras played there. Wrestling matches were also held and Billy Graham preached there. In 1949, ballet arrived at the Embassy for five gala performances, from the end of November to early December. Billed as the world's greatest ballet stars, Alicia Markova and Anton Dolin appeared there along with the corps de ballet and orchestra. The cinema was packed. Staff remember the Emperor of Abyssinia, his wife and children visiting the cinema one night while they were residing in Bath.

The Embassy's demise came in 1963. It was just too big to survive. The cinema ended by hosting a run of Greta Garbo films that attracted very good audiences. It was later demolished; the building that replaced it was named Embassy House in its honour.

EMBASSY CLIFTON BRISTOL

*Mon. and Wed.*
*November 28th and 30th, at 7 p.m.*

*Thurs., Fri and Sat.*
*December 1st, 2nd and 3rd, at 7 p.m.*

JULIAN BRAUNSWEG and VICTOR HOCHHAUSER
(For J.C.A.P.B. Ltd.)

*presents*

# THE BALLET EVENT OF THE YEAR

FIVE GALA PERFORMANCES ONLY

BY

THE WORLD'S GREATEST BALLET STARS

## ALICIA
# MARKOVA
## ANTON
# DOLIN

## WITH CORPS DE BALLET

AND

## THEIR ORCHESTRA

**Conductor:**

## LEIGHTON LUCAS

SPECTACULAR BALLET PRESENTATION

SPECIALLY-CONSTRUCTED STAGE

UNIQUE LIGHTING EFFECTS

**BOOK AT:**

CHARLES H. LOCKIER
CONCERT DIRECTION
29-31 QUEEN'S ROAD, BRISTOL 8
Telephone: 23885

Tickets: 5/-, 7/6, 10/-, 12/6 and 15/-

Opposite: *Ballet at the Embassy in 1949. Dolin and Markova dance for Bristol.*

Right: *The Embassy, c. 1950.*

Below: *The large, luxurious interior of the Embassy, c. 1950.*

# Empire, Old Market, 1931-1939

The Empire Palace of Varieties, to give it its full name, opened in 1893 to serve the people of East Bristol. Some of the greatest stars of the day appeared there under the management of Sid Macaire, including Flanagan and Allen, Belle Ellmore (later the wife and victim of the infamous Dr Crippen), Marie Lloyd, Gracie Fields, Old Mother Riley (Arthur Lucan) and Harry Houdini, to name but a few. Archibald Leach, who later became Cary Grant, once worked there, operating the arch lights; it was one of his earliest jobs.

The Empire became a cinema in 1931. Its first film was a talkie, *The Taming of the Shrew*, with Mary Pickford and Douglas Fairbanks. The new cinema was advertised as 'Bristol's new supercinema' but it wasn't all plain sailing. In May 1932, they were fined £5 for allowing children to attend an 'A' certificate film. It was said that 200 children under the age of sixteen had watched the film. In the same year, the ABC group took over the cinema. By that time, Bristol had so many picture houses it was reaching saturation point and by 1937 some live entertainment was being presented at the Empire again. In 1939, it was announced that the cinema would close because of the outbreak of the Second World War. The closure was short-lived but when the Empire reopened, it was as a variety theatre. The theatre closed for good in 1954. Nearby Castle Street had been destroyed in the Blitz and the Old Market area had suffered badly. People were moving out of the area to new estates. The BBC used the building for a short time and then Bristol City Council purchased it, demolishing it as part of the Old Market roundabout scheme in 1964.

*The Empire Palace of Varieties. Patrons usually entered via the White Hart Hotel in Old Market Street.*

*The entrance to the Empire can be seen on the left, next to the Empire Stores. The rest of the building was in Carey's Lane, around the corner. The bus on the right has stopped where the Olympia cinema stood.*

*Staff at the Empire, c. 1936.*

# Europa, Castle Street, 1973-1987

The Europa opened quietly in 1973; there was no big opening event as in the past. The cinema was situated at the end of the Holiday Inn Hotel in Castle Street. It closed in 1987 and twelve members of staff lost their jobs.

# Fishponds Picture House, 1911-1926

Fishponds Picture House was built by John Edmond Blake, a foreman printer who lived at No. 43 Lodge Causeway. The cinema was built at the junction of Station Road and Fishponds Road, on an empty plot of land. John Blake's licence ran from 6 February 1911, which may have been the date the cinema opened. Fishponds was at that time almost a village, so the cinema catered for local people. John Blake offered money from the cinema to St John's church in Lodge Causeway but they refused. For some reason, the church regarded the cinema with some suspicion. However, they accepted the money from Mr Blake's own pocket.

In 1913, the Fishponds Picture House was sold to Henry John Davey, who was an optician by trade, for a total of £700. In 1921, he sold it to Herbert Wren, who already owned the Regal in Staple Hill. He in turn sold it to Sid Macaire in the following year, on the condition that he didn't open another cinema between Fishponds and the Regal. Sid Macaire had had quite a distinguished career already: from around 1906 to 1919, he had been the manager of the Empire in Old Market. The insurance on the Fishponds Picture House for 1925/26 was £1 18s for three months and it was insured for £4,000 to cover the entrance office, the operating room and hall and the piano.

Mr Macaire heard rumours that a more modern cinema, the Vandyck, was being built in Fishponds and he knew that he wouldn't be able to compete, so before the Vandyck opened in November 1926, he sold the Fishponds Picture House to Bristol City Council on 7 August 1926 for £2,500. The council turned the building into a library. They did a lot of work renovating it, building an extension to the side to be used as an office, kitchen, restroom and toilet. They also changed the entrance, moving it to Station Road. The library consisted of three departments: a lending library for adults, a general reading room and a children's room. It opened to the public in December 1927. In 1960, the entrance was moved back to the front of the building, on Fishponds Road. Local people often don't believe that the library was once a cinema and often ask if it was a church, as it has that look about it.

Opposite above: *A Loxton drawing of the Fishponds Picture House, c. 1911. The church to the left is still standing and is now used as a car showroom.*

Opposite middle: *Fishponds Picture House.*

Opposite below: *The picture house is now Fishponds Library, seen here in 2005.*

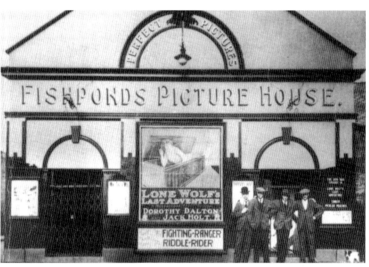

# Gaiety, Wells Road, 1933–1995

The Gaiety was built on the corner of what was known as Crossways, on the site of a former limekiln. It was built and owned by Roy Chamberlain, who lived in the house next door. After the builders had left the site each day, Roy's children would take to the stage, pretending that they had an audience. Despite opposition to the cinema from the local community and the local church, who feared it would change the character of the area, the Gaiety opened on Boxing Day 1933 at 2 p.m., the same day as the News Theatre.

The Gaiety was described at the time as having been 'designed in a plain but dignified style' and seated 800. The operating box was fitted with two Kalee 8 projectors. The whole cinema was carpeted in a two-tone brown carpet, bought in a job lot when Bobby's was taken over by Bright's. Roy even used it in his own house, much to his wife's horror! The heating was underneath the floor of the auditorium and there was a dance hall on the balcony floor that could accommodate 125 people.

The cinema's most striking feature was its fine wall paintings. The theme of the paintings was the landing of Charles I in Morocco and the scene above the balcony showed tree-covered hills with white domes and minarets gleaming among the foliage. The outstanding features of the scene were two large galleons flying the flag of England. The paintings were the work of well-known cinema artist George Legge.

The first film shown at the Gaiety was *Good Companions*, starring Jessie Matthews, Edmund Gwenn and John Gielgud. Fifty years later, they showed the same film and received a nice letter of congratulation from Jessie.

The cinema was lucky to survive the Second World War, as the large, white building was an easy target. Incendiary bombs landed on the roof but luckily burnt themselves out. After the war, Roy's son Denys took over; he had known cinema all his life. His father continued in local politics, becoming Lord Mayor in 1958.

In 1966, *The Sound of Music* ran for five weeks and was completely sold out, despite the fact that the film had already run for months in town. In 1983, the Gaiety received an award for fifty years of continuous exhibition. In 1991, Denys became the chairman of the National Cinematograph Exhibitors. It was at this time that he sold the picture house. It could no longer compete with the new supercinemas and closed in 1995. Several fires on the site made the building unsafe and it was finally demolished in 2000, with local MP Dawn Primorolo helping to knock it down. Sheltered housing now stands in its place. In November 2003, a blue plaque was unveiled to mark where the Gaiety once stood.

It is said that over 8 million filmgoers passed through the Gaiety's doors. Cary Grant once visited; he came alone and was quietly welcomed by the manager, as he had wished. Bob Monkhouse was another famous visitor; while playing at Weston-super-Mare, he telephoned to say that he wanted to see a film he had missed and was also welcomed with no fuss. Leslie Crowther also made a visit.

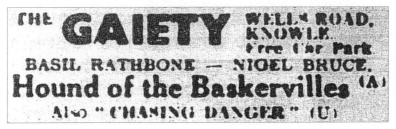

*An advertisement for* Hound of the Baskervilles, *showing at the Gaiety.*

Right: *The Gaiety before its revamp.*

Below: *The car from the film* Chitty Chitty Bang Bang *visiting the Gaiety for a publicity event.*

*Walt Disney characters publicise a Disney Summer Festival at the Gaiety. Denys Chamberlain organised this festival, which soon became an annual event.*

*The Gaiety.*

*The Gaiety after its closure, a sad end for a great cinema.*

*Flats have now been built on the site of the Gaiety. In 2003, a blue plaque was unveiled to commemorate the cinema. From left to right: Denys Chamberlain, ex-owner; Wally Ball, ex-projectionist and cinema historian and Bill Martin, Lord Mayor of Bristol.*

# Gem, No. 7 Broadweir, c. 1909–1932

This was one of the earliest cinemas in Bristol and was another of the old music hall theatres. It was previously known as the Broadweir and the Vaudeville Theatre. When it became a cinema, the building was totally refurbished, a sculpted frontage was added and the name was changed to the Gem Electric Theatre, known simply as the Gem. It was situated in Broadweir, which ran from Merchant Street to Ellbroad Street. At No.3 was the famous Berkeley Restaurant, owned by Sam J. Money.

The Gem was owned by A.F. Moon, who later built the Whiteladies in Clifton and the Regent in Kingswood. It was one of the last Bristol picture houses to go over to the talkies because, even though it had three floors and seated 1,200 people, it just wasn't big enough for all the equipment necessary for sound. The Gem hung on for as long as possible, in the hope that the talkies would be a five-minute wonder, but in the end the supply of silent films dried up and they had no choice but to convert. This wasn't easy, as the projection box had to be extended to accommodate the equipment. The beam shone in through the circle, so that if someone walked past the beam it would show up on the screen, much to everyone's annoyance.

The Gem was always considered to be a bit of a fleapit, with its hard benches nailed to the floor. It closed in 1932 and soon became a boxing club. There had been boxing matches held there in the past. On 12 February 1934, Jimmy Cooper, who was not quite fifteen years old, collapsed and died there after being knocked down in an unlicensed fight. The other boxer was just twenty-two years old and the coroner expressed many concerns. The boxing club closed and the building became run-down, with further damage being sustained during the Blitz of 1940.

GEM THEATRE,
BROADWEIR.   Continuous, 2.30 till 10.15 p.m.
TO-DAY (MON.), TUESDAY and WEDNESDAY.
REX DAVIS and EVA MOORE in
"MOTHERLAND."
And VERA REYNOLDS in "MILITARY MAIDS."
Serial: "BELPHEGOR."

*An advertisement for* Motherland *at the Gem.*

*The Gem in its early days.*

# Globe, Church Road, Lawrence Hill, 1914-1973

In order to build the Globe, a few houses in Jane Street and two shops on Church Road were demolished. It was built and owned by Joseph Pugsley, who also owned the scrapyard at the rear of the cinema. He was blind, so couldn't watch the films; his eldest son George made all the arrangements for him, under his supervision.

The Globe opened on 26 March 1914. The programme for the opening day promised 'an all-star programme including one of the most sensational films ever produced'. The film was *The Baboon's Vengeance or The Conscience of the Great Unknown*, 'exclusive to this hall for 3 days only'. The programme also stated that 'the Globe orchestra will render music appropriate to each picture'. The cinema had an eight- or nine-piece orchestra but for matinees only the piano was used. It was usually played by Elsie Holland, who had once played for Randolph Sutton.

The Globe could seat 1,172 people. On both sides of the auditorium were murals showing scenes from the Great Fire of London. Over the years, nicotine stained these pictures and made them difficult to see. There was a small lavatory inside for ladies, and an outside one for gentlemen. There was a covered queuing area in Jane Street.

During the First World War, the manager, Mr John, was called up. On his return, staff and locals put up banners saying 'Welcome home, Mr John'. There was no first-name familiarity in those days.

In June 1916, a touch of Hollywood came to the Globe when Miss Lillian Lorraine, star of the silent film *The Girl of Lost Island*, paid a visit. Special publicity cards were printed and there were huge crowds outside.

The Globe showed its last silent film on Saturday 23 November 1929 and opened as a talkie cinema on Monday 25 November. The orchestra members were no longer required. The first talkie shown was a very primitive version of *Showboat*, not to be confused with the 1936 version. The cinema's takings doubled. In the week ending 8 February 1930, 15,024 people came to see *The Desert Song*; the total money taken was £660 0s 5½d.

Joseph Pugsley died just before the advent of the talkies. Oliver Pugsley took over the cinema and George took over the scrap-metal business. By that time, the Pugsleys also ran the Queen's and St George's Hall picture houses.

Advertising was always a problem at the Globe because there were so many competitors. In 1933, when *The Invisible Man* was showing, the manager needed a gimmick. He put a fish tank in the foyer, filled it with water but didn't put any fish in it. He put a sign on the tank which read 'Come and see the invisible fish'. Word got around and people came just to see this fish tank. The staff were amazed when people actually asked where the invisible fish were!

Just before the Second World War, the cinema was given a revamp. The very ornate pillars disappeared and the building lost its character. The doors now came out almost to the pavement and new seats were fitted.

Jack E. Wyard was the manager there for many years. He had started as a projectionist at the nearby Granada. He was always very well dressed and expected his staff to look smart too. The cinema was his life.

Things went downhill during the 1950s and early 1960s, as people moved away from the district. There were also problems with gangs of youths; the manager was stabbed on one occasion as he tried to avert trouble. In its last days, *Goldfinger* and *Hang 'em High* together brought in only 708 people, with takings of just £260.60. The last film shown at the Globe was Walt Disney's *Aristocats* on 6 January 1973. The cinema was demolished to make way for City Motors.

Above left and right: *Two advertisements for 'The New Globe'.*

*An early photograph of the Globe.*

Above: *The interior of the Globe.*

Right: *Steve James on the roof of the Globe cinema. During the Second World War, Steve was almost killed when he went to nearby Lawrence Hill station to collect a film. A bomb dropped nearby but luckily Steve was pulled to the ground by a member of the railway staff. He returned to the Globe, shaken and without the film. Steve started out as a rewind boy at the Globe, and was later promoted to projectionist. He met his future wife at the cinema and they are still happily married.*

*The Globe had a canopy on the Jane Street side of the building to shelter queuing filmgoers.*

*The Globe in the 1970s, in the final days before it was demolished.*

*Joseph Pugsley, owner of the Globe, with his wife Mary.*

*Joseph Pugsley and his second wife, Mary Ann (née Collier), with son Oliver and daughter Winifred, around the time of the First World War.*

Above: *The Pugsley boys. Oliver and William are at the back and Fred, Edward and George in front. George and William were twins.*

Left: *Oliver Pugsley.*

Below: *The annual outing of staff from the Globe and the Granada. Cecil Ashford, manager of the Granada, and Jack Wyard, manager of the Globe, are at the back. The group includes Oliver and Alice Pugsley, with their children Beryl and Mary, and Kathleen Fitzpatrick.*

# Hippodrome/Stoll, East Street, Bedminster, 1915-1941

The Hippodrome was situated in East Street, between Essex Street and Lombard Street. It opened as a music hall in July 1911, owned by Walter de Fleece. It was a very wide, beautiful building with two enormous side turrets, a large canopy and broad white steps. Unfortunately, De Fleece ran into money problems and had to sell. In stepped Mr Stoll, who had built the Hippodrome in St Augustine's Parade. He converted the music hall to a cinema in May 1915 and, always one for self-publicity, renamed it the Stoll Picture Theatre, known locally as the Stoll. An unusual feature of the cinema was its orchestrated organ. Sometimes the cinema put on a variety act between films; Tessie O'Shea and Randolph Sutton both performed there.

Russ Conway, the great pop pianist of the 1950s and '60s, came to this picture house as a young lad. He recalled occasions when a distraught manager had to shut down a film because of problems, leaving a well-lit but blank screen. The film usually came back but while they were waiting there was a huge amount of noise from people shouting and stamping their feet, and the manager would tell them to shut up.

The Stoll received a direct hit during the bombing on 3 January 1941 and was destroyed.

*The Hippodrome, which was renamed the Stoll Picture Theatre.*

The **STOLL** PICTURE THEATRE, *To-day*
BEDMINSTER. *Continuous* 3 till 10.30

At 3.35 — 6.5 — 8.40.

RAMON NOVARRO and ALICE TERRY in

" S C A R A M O U C H E "

The Film that Smashed all London Theatre Records.

JIMMY and ETHEL CLARK, Somewhat Different Dancers. At 5.20 and 7.55.
Thursday Next: "RIDERS OF THE DARK."

*An advertisement for* Scaramouche *at the Stoll, formerly the Hippodrome in Bedminster.*

*The Bedminster Hippodrome.*

# Hippodrome, No. 309 Stapleton Road, Eastville, 1913-1959

Designed by W.H. Watkins and owned by George Allen, who also owned His Majesty's and the Metropole, the Hippodrome seated just 300, with some double seats for courting couples. It was one of the smallest cinemas in Bristol. The screen was at the entrance end of the building, so people had to walk in sideways, edging themselves into a seat. It was not one of Watkins' better designs but it was cheap and cheerful, which is probably what the owners wanted. The staff wore uniforms which had 'E.H.' for Eastville Hippodrome embroidered on them. The cinema closed in 1959 and the building, now part of the Bristol Trading Centre, is still standing today.

*The Eastville Hippodrome.*

Right: *Jim Hiscox, an attendant at Eastville Hippodrome, wearing his uniform.*

Below: *An advertisement for* Palais de Danse *at the Hippodrome.*

Bottom: *Eastville Hippodrome, 2005.*

## HIS MAJESTY'S
EASTVILLE.     6.0—CONTINUOUS—10.30.
TO-DAY (MON.), TUESDAY and WEDNESDAY.
NORMA SHEARER in
### "THE LATEST FROM PARIS,"
A charming love story played in a delightful Comedy vein.
MATINEES: Mon., Wed., Thurs., Sat. at 2.45.
Thursday Next: KARL DANE and GEORGE
K. ARTHUR in " CIRCUS ROOKIES."

## THE METROPOLE
ASHLEY ROAD.     6.0—CONTINUOUS—10.30
TO-DAY (MON.), TUESDAY and WEDNESDAY.
BEBE DANIELS in
### "FEEL MY PULSE,"
Love, Life and Laughter.
Thursday Next: MARION DAVIES and CON-
RAD NAGEL in "QUALITY STREET."

### EASTVILLE HIPPODROME: "PALAIS DE DANSE."

# His Majesty's/Concorde, No. 424 Stapleton Road, 1911-1990

This cinema opened in 1911 as Jesty's Picture Palace but was soon renamed His Majesty's. It was owned by George Allen, who also owned the nearby Eastville Hippodrome and the Metropole. The three cinemas were close together and could be reached quickly by a film boy on a bicycle if they needed to swap films. When it was built, it seated 800, which was almost three times the size of the Eastville Hippodrome. At this time, Stapleton Road was a very well-to-do area.

George Allen carried out a major refurbishment in the late 1930s. The whole building was smartened up and a balcony added. The cinema could now seat 1,150. It was also at this time that Allen built the Carlton (1933) and the Ritz (1938).

Allen died in the late 1950s and his wife continued to run the business for a while before deciding to sell up. In 1969, it was sold to the Northern Star group. They wanted to turn the cinema into a bingo hall with two small cinema screens but the council rejected their plans because there was insufficient parking space. Northern Star won an appeal and the building reopened as the Concorde in 1973. It made the national press in 1990 when just one customer came to see *The Emerald Forest* in cinema 1 and no one at all came to cinema 2. The customer was asked if he would come back another night but it was the last night for that particular film. He went to the press.

The Concorde closed in 1990 and became a furniture warehouse.

*His Majesty's cinema in Stapleton Road.*

*The Concorde EMI Bingo and Social Club.*

*The old cinema is now Concorde Furnishings.*

# Hotwells Cinema Theatre, Hotwells Road, 1915-1939

Hotwells Cinema Theatre was situated on Hotwells Road, between Avon Square and Ambra Vale. William James Ashford's shop was on one side and the Spring Garden Hotel on the other. The cinema was built to cater for Clifton Wood and the old dockside areas and seated 450 in a single-storey building. In its early days, the proprietor was Sidney John Champion. In 1925, it was T. Channing. In 1937, A.P. Atkinson was the lessee and general manager. The cinema closed in 1939.

**HOTWELLS CINEMA THEATRE,**

S. J. CHAMPION.
Proprietor.

Bristol, Oct 29 1918

This is to say that Leonard Hooper has been in my employ for the last 6 months as assistant Operator & I can thoroughly recommend him.

S J Champion

Right: *A reference written for a member of staff at the Hotwells Cinema Theatre, 1918.*

Below: *The site of the Hotwells Cinema Theatre as it was in the 1980s.*

Equipu P.L.C.    For all Office equipment

# King's, Old Market Street, 1911-1976

British Electric Theatres owned this small cinema, which was originally called King's Hall. It was built on the site of a cemetery, between Old Market Street and Redcross Street, and when it was demolished, bones from the cemetery were discovered and removed. It was British Electric Theatres who put a test case for Sunday opening in 1910. The inspector went to another cinema, saw some nudity and a scene in which a vicar kissed a woman and promptly objected. The case was refused.

After the First World War, Ralph Bromhead, who was later a leading light in the Gaumont empire, took over the King's and changed it beyond recognition. He purchased the shop next door and gave the building a new frontage, with a wide foyer and low canopy outside. Inside, the balcony area was decorated with ornate brasswork. In order to obtain planning permission, Bromhead had to employ fifty demobilised men as labourers. The work took less than a year and cost £15,000. The King's reopened in 1921 and became a landmark in Old Market Street.

The cinema suffered a fire in 1926 but soon reopened with new owners, Enrico Carreras and his son James. They had their own orchestra, the King's Symphony Orchestra, consisting of twelve musicians. The orchestra played twice a day every day and were paid £68 per week between them, which was better than most musicians were paid at that time.

The King's cinema's biggest competitor was the Regent in nearby Castle Street. A gimmick was needed to put the King's in front, so they took a gamble and tried the talkies. They were the first in Bristol to do this and changed the face of Bristol cinema for ever. In March 1929, they opened with the film *The Singing Fool*, starring Al Jolson. The queues went all the way up Old Market Street and they packed in four performances a day for five weeks. They counted 50,000 admissions in the first two weeks, figures unheard of before. It was the end for silent films.

By the end of the 1930s, the ABC Group, under John Maxwell, had taken over the cinema and it continued to be popular. It survived the Second World War but the surrounding area and, following the redevelopment of the area and the building of the new road system, the cinema became isolated. It closed on 4 December 1976 with a double bill of *Hot Dreams* and *Man Hungry*. This once great cinema was eventually demolished and an office block built on the site.

**Tele.: 4623.**

# Kings
**BRISTOL**

## OLD MARKET STREET
### THE HOME OF THE "TALKIES."

### TO-DAY.

Paramount Great Talkie Film,

## "The Doctor's Secret"
WITH
### RUTH CHATTERTON
AND
### H. B. WARNER

Adapted from Sir J. M. Barrie's Play,
"Half an Hour."
The Sunday Dispatch Says:—
"The Best Talkie yet."

Four Distinct and Separate Performances Daily:
**1.30, 3.45, 6.0, and 8.15.**
Doors Open at 1.0 p.m.
Seats Booked for all Performances at 2/4 only.

Box Office Open Daily from 10.30 a.m.
Seats Booked by 'Phone must be claimed
10 minutes before commencement of
Performance

Above: *An advertisement for a film showing at the King's.*

Right: *An advertisement for a film featuring Rudolph Valentino, the heart throb of the 1920s. There was huge scale grief and hysteria when he died in 1926 aged just thirty-one.*

Opposite: *The King's after it had been taken over by ABC.*

# KINGS
## CINEMA
### OLD MARKET STREET

## CONTINUOUS
## PERFORMANCES
### DAILY OF
# RUDOLPH
# VALENTINO
### IN
## "MONSIEUR
## BEAUCAIRE"
APPROXIMATELY AT
# 2.30, 5.30 and 8.30.
PRECEDED BY A NOVEL AND
### ORIGINAL PROLOGUE
FEATURING
### VERA BARGUS (Ballet)
### REG. BRIMBLE (Baritone).

### Three Distinct
### Performances
### on Saturday.

## FREE & SAFE GARAGE
### for Patrons' Cars.

## MAY 18th, For One Week,
SPECIAL ENGAGEMENT
AND *PERSONAL VISIT* OF
# OLLY OAKLEY,
### THE WORLD'S GREATEST
## BANJO VIRTUOSO
OF
### GRAMOPHONE RECORD AND
### B.B.C. FAME.

BRISTOL'S NATURAL BEAUTY·SPOT **THE GLEN** DURDHAM DOWN
DAILY AT 3 0 & 7·30 WET or FINE
ALL THIS WEEK, the FAMOUS
## MEXICAN BAND.
Direct from Olympia, London.
PRICES AS USUAL.

Right: *In 1927, this unemployed man walked from London to Bristol to advertise the film* Tramp, Tramp, Tramp *at the King's cinema. His reward was £5. His boots were supplied by the Bristol firm Lennard's.*

Below: *The King's in its last days.*

# Kingsway, No. 93 Two Mile Hill, 1928-1959

The Kingsway opened in 1928. It cost £9,000 to build and seated 800 people. It had a covered way on one side which was used as a car park but it could only hold four or five cars. The projection box was made of concrete with iron shutters. At the interval, these clanged shut and the noise reverberated around the auditorium.

In the 1930s, the owners were England and Burnham and the manager was W. Tudor Ballard. In the 1940s, Bruce Atkinson and his partner Mr Rees took over (see Zetland Road, the Dolphin, the Vestry, the Redcliffe, Bedminster Town Hall, the Plaza and the Scala). This was Bruce's last cinema; he died in 1948. During the 1950s, John Crewe was the manager. He is remembered for standing outside in his evening suit, rocking on his heels and saying, '1s 9d to the left, 2s 3d to the right.' He showed 'blue' films on Sunday mornings to a men-only audience. There were no advertisements, just word of mouth.

The Kingsway closed in 1959 and became a car showroom. The sloping floor of the auditorium had to be levelled out with tons of concrete, and huge power tools were needed to remove the projection box. Strangely enough, one of the original fluorescent light fittings has survived and can still be seen just inside the door, and the balcony is also still intact. There are plans to turn the building into flats, retaining the frontage.

*The Kingsway, 1950s.*

*Kingsway Motors Ltd. Many cinema buffs have visited this former picture house and been given a tour by its owner.*

*Inside the car showroom, looking down from the old balcony of the cinema, 2004.*

*The cinema's balcony can still be seen in the car showroom, 2004.*

*One of the Kingsway's original light fittings, 2004.*

# Knowle Picture House, Nos 109-111 Wells Road, 1913-1961

W.H. Watkins designed the Knowle Picture House and it is probably one of his best cinemas, although it was thought to be a little too ornate. It had two windows based on a pineapple design, with three pillars in between. Behind the pillars was the window of the billiard room. The foyer was almost as big as the auditorium and above the screen were two beautiful cherubs.

In the first year of trading, the owners – two businessmen – showed a loss of £379, and they made a two-year profit of just £66. Six years later, in 1919, the Knowle Picture House was in the hands of the receivers. Roy Chamberlain, who had tried to lease Bedminster Town Hall but had been beaten to it by Ralph Pringle, rented it for three years at £7 per week. In 1922, he bought the cinema for £8,300. He raised the roof to enable a balcony to be added, which may well have spoilt the look of the building. The Chamberlain family, who also owned the sweet shop next door to the cinema, had, in the words of Denys Chamberlain, 'years of success but then years of failure' and the Knowle Picture House closed in 1961. It was later demolished.

*The Knowle Picture House.*

Right: *W.H. Watkins' original design for the Knowle Picture House.*

Below: *An advertisement for Carefree, starring Fred Astaire and Ginger Rogers.*

KNOWLE PICTURE HOUSE
FRED ASTAIRE — GINGER ROGERS.
CAREFREE (U)

BROADWAY FILWOOD PARK.
KNOWLE.
Ralph RICHARDSON Valerie HOBSON.
Q PLANES
U
also 'LITTLE ADVENTURESS' (U)

# Magnet, Nos 51-53 Newfoundland Street, 1914-1937

In 1914, William Wensley bought Nos 51-53 Newfoundland Street and Nos 23-24 Orange Street, which were directly behind. He then knocked the buildings through and created the Magnet cinema. The sub classical, or Edwardian classical, design was by Holbrow and Oaten, who specialised in small cinemas. It had heavy architraves and apron panel segmental arches and could seat 520 people. In 1919, it was sold to William S. Chamberlain (*see* the Gaiety, the Knowle Picture House and the Broadway).

Ernest Davies started out there as a trainee projectionist. He had been the film boy at the St George's Hall picture house and was known as 'Curly' Davies. He later worked at many Bristol cinemas, eventually becoming a manager. He was manager at the Globe when it closed in 1973.

Many people remember hearing the sounds of pig's trotters being eaten in the Magnet – they were a popular local delicacy, sold at Brittan's pork butchers in nearby Wade Street. After the film, many people went for a drink in the Foundry Inn, the Rising Sun or the Carpenters' Arms.

Slum clearance in the 1930s led to the closure of the Magnet. It closed in 1937 and was sold to C.A. Roberts. In the 1950s, dairy products and frozen foods were packed there. It was later used by Golding's, who sold office equipment. Today it is the home of building contractors C.W. Duke & Sons Ltd.

*The Magnet cinema.*

*The Magnet as it looks today, 2005.*

*The rear of the former Magnet cinema remains unchanged.*

# Metropole, Ashley Road, 1913-1968

The Metropole was built on the site of Criterion Cottages in Ashley Road. In its day, it was a simple but effective single-storey cinema, fronted by a large courtyard. It opened in 1913 and seated 600 people.

Cary Grant, one of the great stars of cinema, was born in Bristol and lived with his father and grandmother near the Metropole, at No. 21 Picton Street. He was known then as Archibald Leach and attended Fairfield Grammar School, from where he was expelled. According to one of Grant's biographers, he went with his father to the Metropole to see the silent films of the day, especially the slapstick comedies like *The Keystone Cops* that he loved so much. Grant remembered the Metropole as 'a barn-like building with hard seats and bare floors, where all the men smoked'. He also mentions visits to Pringle's Palace (the Scala) and to the Clare Street Picture House (*see* also the Gaiety).

In 1938, owner George Allen commissioned W.H. Watkins to redesign and modernise the Metropole. Ashley Road was at that time a very wealthy area and the cinema was regularly filled to capacity, so Allen decided to enlarge it. The old building was completely altered: the courtyard disappeared and the building now came out to the pavement. The refurbished cinema, which was renamed the Metropole De Luxe, seated 1,460 and had a balcony, plush seating and carpets and a foyer that patrons would linger in. There was also a tea room with glass-topped tables and Lloyd Loom chairs.

The Metropole closed in 1968, when it was sold to the Northern Star Group. They converted the cinema into a bingo hall, although it continued to show films on Sundays. In 1979, Derek Cooper and his wife tried to reopen the Metropole as a cinema but on two occasions wreckers got in, causing a great deal of damage. It became a furniture warehouse and was later demolished. Wally Ball, former silent film projectionist and cinema historian, watched as the cinema was bulldozed. He had been given his first job at the Metropole in 1927. He said, 'In a way I'm pleased to see it go as it has become an eyesore, but yes, that's tinged with sadness ... you could say they are closing down my cinema.' A bank and new flats known as Ashley Court now stand on the site.

*An advertisement for* Gunga Din *at the Metropole.*

Above: *The Metropole before it was enlarged.*

Right: *The Metropole in use as a bingo hall.*

# ℂews Theatre, Peter Street, 1933-1956

The News Theatre was built to replace the Queen's Picture House and stood on the same site at the top of Castle Street. It was opposite St Peter's church and close to the Bear and Rugged Staff and the Fox pubs. Next door was Lakers oyster bar, where there were no seats, just a bar where you stood and ate shellfish.

The opening ceremony took place on 26 December 1933, the same day as the Gaiety. The Lord Mayor of Bristol, Mr F.C. Luke, performed the opening ceremony without actually being there on the day. He was unable to attend due to prior engagements so he was filmed making the opening speech and this was shown on the screen. The Lord Mayor welcomed Mr J. Cohen's enterprise.

The News Theatre was designed by W.H. Watkins and built by Frank Wilkins of Lawford's Gate, who had a long association with Watkins. The building had a very striking frontage, something new for Bristol and for Watkins. The whole of the main façade was faced with black and steel bands, the tower rising above the main entrance was faced with black and the flanking walls with horizontal bands of green and black glass on a granite base. The interior had a delicate colour scheme of peach, pale green and silver, with walnut doors, pale green architraves and black skirting.

The cinema could seat 400. It had a parcel depository, an information bureau and a nursery where children were looked after while their parents watched the film or went shopping, all included in the admission price of 6d or 1s for a one-hour programme. There was a continuous programme from 12.30 p.m to 11 p.m. The news was the main feature, although nature, travel, art, fashion and comedy items were also screened. The only films shown were 'U' certificate, mostly Walt Disney films.

In November 1940, the News Theatre was damaged in an air raid but it reopened on 23 December. The nearby Regent wasn't so lucky: Castle Street was devastated and the Regent, in oppsite Peter Street, was one of the buildings that was destroyed. After the bombing, the News Theatre stood almost entirely on its own. It closed in 1956 and stood empty for three years before finally being demolished as part of the redevelopment of the Castle Street area.

*The Queen's Picture House, which was replaced by the News Theatre.*

## NEWS THEATRE
(Top of Castle Street.)

The Most Popular House of Entertainment in Bristol.

MONDAY, FEBRUARY 14th & during the week

## LAUREL
### AND
## HARDY
## Comedy
## Week!!!

including Two of their most laughable
and exhilarating Comedies ever made

"TIT FOR TAT" and "THE FIXER UPPERS"

"TWO TOO YOUNG" Comedy by "OUR GANG"
"PLUTO'S QUIN-PUPLETS" Disney's Latest Cartoon.

☞ AND ALL THE NEWS ☜

**6d.** A Scream from beginning to end **1/-**

TWO PRICES ONLY

Right: *An advertisement for Laurel and Hardy Comedy Week.*

Below: *The Queen's Picture House before it was replaced by the News Theatre.*

*The cinema was damaged by enemy bombing during the Second World War but soon reopened.*

*The News Theatre.*

# Odeon, Union Street, 1938-present

When the Odeon in Union Street opened on 16 July 1938, owner Oscar Deutsch claimed it was 'the finest cinema in the country'. Deutsch owned lots of cinemas, many of which looked alike. The Odeon was formally opened by Lord Apsley, with the Royal Marine Artillery Mounted Band providing the music. The opening film was *Mad About Music*, starring Deanna Durbin and Herbert Marshall.

The cinema was built on the site of J.S. Fry & Sons' No. 5 chocolate factory, a five-storey building which dated back to 1889 and was finished in Cornish granite. Fry's moved to a new factory at Somerdale, Keynsham in 1921 and the buildings lay empty for a while before being demolished.

The Odeon had a circular, floodlit tower with reflective black armoured-glass windows and a biscuit-coloured exterior, designed by T. Cecil Howitt. Inside were 1,900 seats, 1,000 in the stalls and 900 in the balcony. It is said that Mrs Deutsch was responsible for the interior design. Seating and sight lines were in accordance with the best modern practice and ample legroom was provided. The same high-class seating was fitted throughout the theatre; the position of the seat determined the ticket price.

During the Second World War, incendiary bombs landed on the roof but projectionist Don Cottle climbed up and dealt with them. The cinema was only closed for a few days during wartime, when the river Frome flooded the basement.

On 29 May 1946, the picture house was the scene of a murder. Manager Robert Parrington Jackson was shot twice in his office but no one in the cinema heard the shots, as they coincided with gunshot in the film that was being shown, *The Lights That Failed*. As no money had been stolen, it was widely believed that Jackson was shot by a jealous man. No one was ever arrested and the case remained unsolved until 1989, when a small-time crook by the name of Billy 'The Fish' Fisher confessed to his son on his deathbed. Fisher said that he and Dukey Leonard had travelled from South Wales to rob the cinema but panicked when the manager returned to his office. The police accepted his confession and closed the case.

There have also been reported cases of psychic manifestations in the cinema but they seem to have stopped after the Revd Lionel Fanthorpe and psychic Rosie Malone were called in to investigate.

In 1967, the Odeon was given a major facelift costing £100,000. It was given the largest screen in the city, but the era of the multiscreen cinema was fast approaching and the big screen didn't last long. By 1974, the Odeon had been converted into a multiscreen cinema. The supercinemas on the edge of town were the next threat and in December 1983 the Odeon was gutted and rebuilt at a cost of nearly £4 million. It reopened on 13 June 1985 with the new James Bond film *A View to Kill*. The entrance to the cinema was now much further up the hill in Union Street and the old foyer had become a Mothercare shop.

Many celebrities have visited the cinema over the years, including Kay Kendall, Norman Wisdom and the stars of the 1953 film *Rob Roy*, who attended the premiere there. Thousands of Bristolians will remember seeing *The Sound of Music* at the Odeon. Queues stretched to the top of Union Street and the film ran for over a year, with many people coming back to see it again and again.

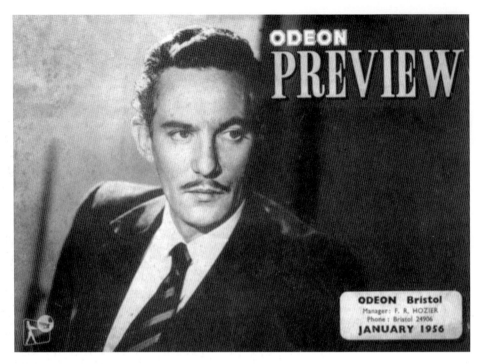

*The* Odeon Preview *contained film news and information about forthcoming films. Peter Finch was the cover star in the January 1956. The manager of the Odeon at that time was F.R. Hozier, who was once manager of the Ambassador at Kingswood.*

*In the 1960s, the queues stretched along Union Street to see* The Sound of Music.

Opposite: *The Odeon before its refit in the 1980s.*

# Olympia/Tatler, Carey's Lane, 1910-1963

This penny gaff cinema opened in 1910 as the Olympia. It had been a roller-skating rink before moving to the more profitable silent movies. Situated in Carey's Lane, off Old Market Street, it could seat 750. It was close to the Empire and the Vestry and was later threatened by the close proximity of the King's. One of its owners was Samuel Justin (*see* the Premier).

After the Second World War, the Olympia closed for modernisation. It was now owned by Jacey's of Birmingham. It reopened on 16 December 1947 under its new name, the Tatler. It had been given a new set of soft seats and, to allow patrons more comfort, it now seated only 560. The colour scheme inside was dove grey, turquoise, pink and white, and there was a very smart café with a small water fountain and walls decorated with cinema posters of the past. It was opened by variety artist Miss Marie Burke, who was playing the principal boy in *Aladdin* at the Theatre Royal.

In 1948, the Tatler changed to showing international films, many with subtitles. The cinema had a large following for these rarely seen films and the management announced that attendance figures had increased considerably. This success didn't last and the cinema closed in 1963. The last film shown was the naturist film *My Bare Lady*, which was billed as 'the newest nudie'.

The last manager of the Tatler was Reg Mills. He started out as a boy working in the Vestry and later worked at the New Palace, the Regent in Castle Street and the Ritz. He was chief operator and then manager at the News Theatre before moving to the Tatler.

Bristol City Council paid £31,000 for the cinema and it was demolished when the inner circuit road and Old Market underpass were built. The contents of the cinema were sold at auction on 19 September 1963, along with some articles from the Empire. Most of the lots went for a few shillings; today they would have been collector's items.

Left: *An advertisement for a double programme at the Tatler.*

Below: *The Tatler used to be called the Olympia.*

Opposite: *The Tatler during its time as a 'continental cinema' showing international films with subtitles.*

Above: *The Tatler in 1950, showing its interesting frontage.*

Right: *A flyer publicising* Femmes de Paris *at the Tatler.*

# Orpheus/Studios Five to Seven/New Orpheus, Northumbria Drive, Henleaze, 1938-present

This was the first cinema built by George Pugsley. He had supervised the building of the Globe, the rebuilding of St George's Hall and the purchase of several other cinemas, being the 'eyes' of his blind father, cinema owner Joseph Pugsley. George's younger brother, Oliver, supervised the running of the Orpheus while George ran the more profitable family scrap-metal business. During the building of the cinema, Oliver had a lucky escape when he fell from the balcony and broke several ribs.

When he built the Orpheus, George Pugsley erected a plaque to William Frieze Greene, a renowned photographer and one of the creators of moving film. In 1921, Pugsley had attended a meeting in London to discuss ways of stemming the flow of American films that were killing the British film industry. An old man got up to speak and suddenly collapsed; it was only then that they discovered it was William Frieze Greene. He was sixty-five years of age, not well dressed and with just 1s 10d in his pocket; many commented that this was exactly the price of a cinema ticket. Pugsley was so touched by the events that he erected a plaque in his memory.

The Orpheus opened on 28 February 1938 with the Frank Capra film *Lost Horizon*, starring Ronald Colman, H.B. Warner and Jane Wyatt. The cinema could seat 1,400, had 17,000ft of floor space and boasted a ceiling that descended in a series of steps. It closed in 1971; the last film to be shown was *Catch 22*. The following year, it was demolished to make way for a supermarket, despite a 500-name petition and a demonstration by children with placards. As a compromise, the owner put in a three-screen mini cinema called Studios Five to Seven. This later closed and reopened as the New Orpheus.

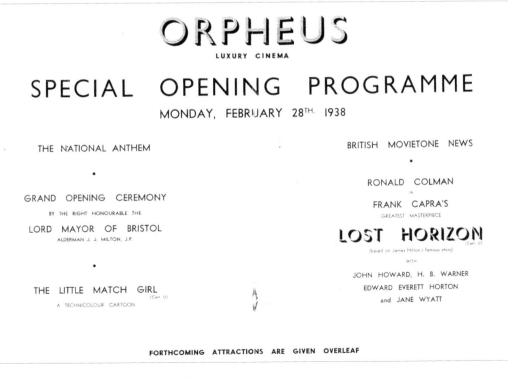

*The opening day programme at the Orpheus.*

Left: *The Orpheus, Henleaze.*

Below: *The cinema's interior.*

Opposite: *One of the many films shown at the Orpheus was* Salome, Where She Danced.

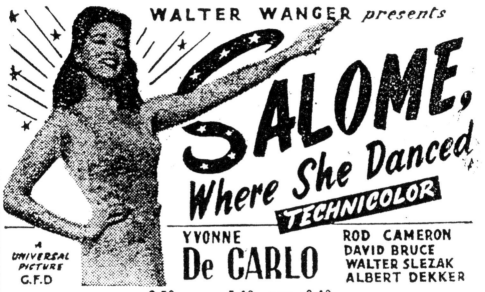

# Park Picture House, Church Road, St George, 1911–1964

The Park Picture House got its name because of its position on the edge of St George's Park. It was another of W.H. Watkins' designs and stood next to the Three Horseshoes pub, which was demolished in 2005.

In the 1920s, a balcony was added to the Park Cinema. This wasn't easy – the back of the building had to be removed for the alterations to take place – but it increased the capacity to 1,020. To reach the fire escape from the rewind and projection room, staff had to scramble up a ladder and through a small glass panel in the roof.

As with many local cinemas, the music was supplied by Hamilton's of Redfield, who gave six records each week in exchange for advertising that appeared on the screen before the film started.

During the Second World War, part of the cinema was used as a base for the local fire-watching team. After the war, Sidney Gamlin (*see* the Cabot and the Vandyck) bought the Park and in the mid-1950s he secured the rights to Cinemascope films after the Odeon group had a disagreement with 20th Century Fox. Gamlin cleaned up the place and spent £8,000 on new equipment, including a big screen that was too big for the small cinema and overlapped onto the side walls. The first film shown after the refit was *The Robe*, the first Cinemascope film, which starred Richard Burton and Jean Simmons.

In the early 1960s, a young courting couple called Chris and Rita were watching a horror film, *The Tingler*, starring Vincent Price. The 'tinglers' of the title are little parasites that can only be removed by screaming. They crawl around under the seats in a cinema. During the film, Chris felt something brush his leg and jumped up screaming. Rita ran from her seat and everyone else turned round to see what was happening. It turned out to be nothing more sinister than the cinema cat.

In 1964, the manager's wife approached Mr Gamlin and told him that her husband was having an affair with a female member of staff. As this was happening in his cinema, Gamlin warned them to end the affair or risk dismissal. The affair continued and so he sacked them both. The rest of the staff protested but he refused to change his mind. In fact he closed the place down and it never reopened. Gamlin was very religious, as was his wife. She had once objected to a poster showing a girl in a bikini that had been put up in the foyer to advertise a popular film.

There were plans to turn the building into a car showroom but planning permission was refused. Gamlin, who was opposed to gambling, would not allow the cinema to become a bingo hall and so, three years after it closed, the cinema was demolished and the site remains empty to this day. It is hard to imagine that there was room for a cinema on this small patch of land.

Above: *The Park in 1964.*

Right: *Sidney Gamlin, owner of the Park, the Cabot and the Vandyck.*

Opposite: *An advertisement for* Brothers *at The Park in 1964.*

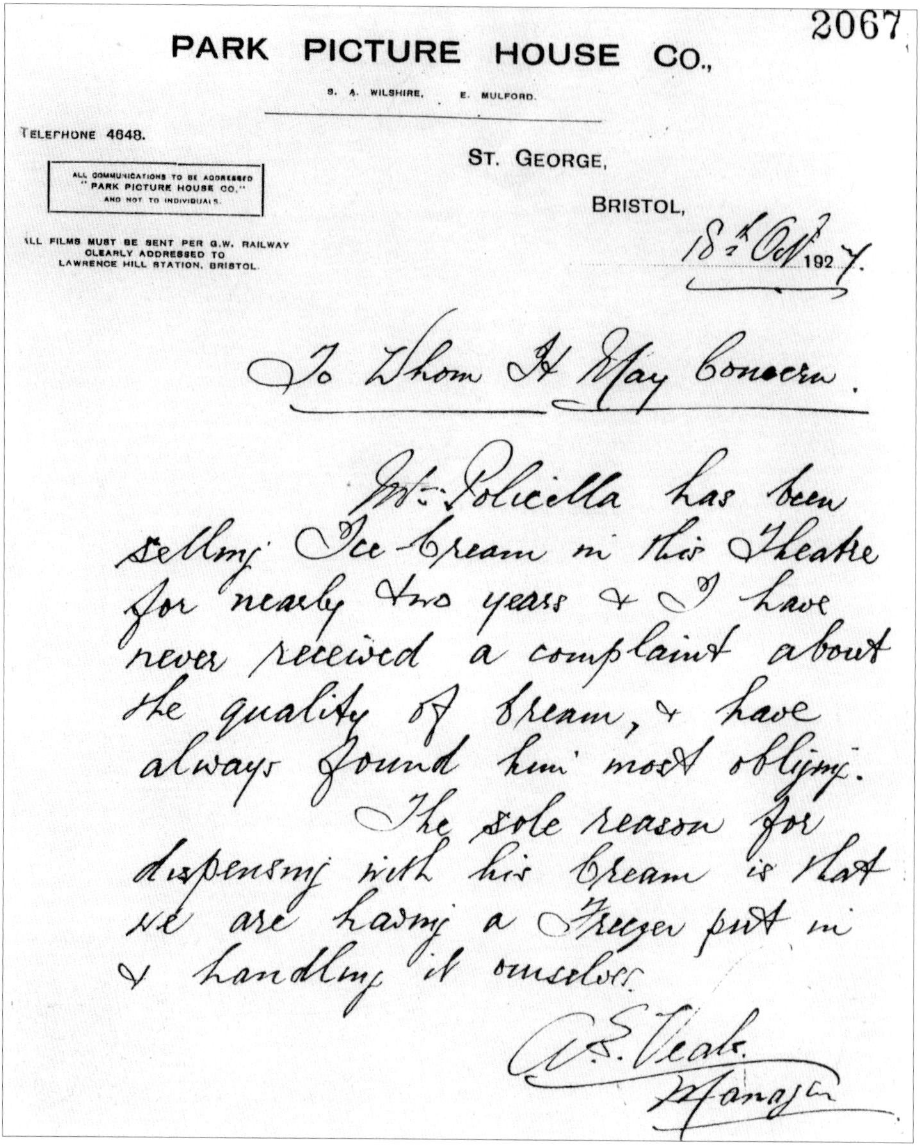

**PARK PICTURE HOUSE CO.,**

S. A. WILSHIRE.    E. MULFORD.

TELEPHONE 4648.

ALL COMMUNICATIONS TO BE ADDRESSED
" PARK PICTURE HOUSE CO."
AND NOT TO INDIVIDUALS.

ALL FILMS MUST BE SENT PER G.W. RAILWAY
CLEARLY ADDRESSED TO
LAWRENCE HILL STATION, BRISTOL.

ST. GEORGE,

BRISTOL,

18th Oct 192 7.

*To Whom It May Concern.*

*Mr. Policella has been selling Ice Cream in this Theatre for nearly two years & I have never received a complaint about the quality of Cream, & have always found him most obliging. The sole reason for dispensing with his Cream is that we are having a Freezer put in & handling it ourselves.*

*W.S. Veale.*
*Manager*

*A reference for Mr Luigi Policella, ice cream seller at the Park, 1927.*

Mr Luigi Policella, an ice cream maker, arrived in England from Italy sometime after 1900. He sold his ice cream in Middlesborough and Hartlepool before serving in the First World War. By 1925, he was living in Bristol, where he made ice cream at home and pushed it up to the Park cinema for sale. Two years later, the Park bought its own freezer and Policella then worked at the King's and the Vandyck. Sometimes his daughter Yolanda would sell the ice cream. In 1930, Policella was back at the Park and also had a shop at No. 26 Malborough Street, St James. In later life, he could often be seen selling ice cream around the tramway centre.

# People's Palace/New Palace/Gaumont, Baldwin Street, 1912-1980

The People's Palace opened as a music hall in 1892. It was designed by James Hutton for the famous Livermore brothers and it is said that there was a well under the stage which belonged to the old Ship and Castle pub that once stood on the site. Many of the stars of the day appeared at the Palace, including Marie Lloyd, George Formby and Charlie Chaplin, who was at that time part of the Eight Lancashire Lads.

An early film was shown at the People's Palace in 1896, as part of the first cinematograph exhibition by the Lumière brothers, and the Palace officially opened as a cinema in 1912. The Livermore brothers sold the cinema in 1920 and in 1927 it was sold again to the Gaumont British Picture Corporation, who completely refurbished it. The cinema could now seat 1,600, with every seat commanding an excellent view of the screen, and had a very steep balcony. There was also a stylish café. The front of the cinema was floodlit by twelve coloured beams of light, designed by Frank Thomas Verity. As well as having its own orchestra, the new cinema also had a three-manual organ on a console that could rise to stage level. The organ had over 100 stops and was equipped with lots of the latest cinema sound effects, such as sirens, whistles, xylophones, glockenspiels and tubular bells. It regularly featured in BBC radio programmes and when it was no longer needed at the cinema it was moved to St Francis' church, Ashton.

The refurbished People's Palace was renamed the New Palace. It was opened on 14 February 1928 by the Lord Mayor of Bristol, Councillor J. Curle JP. The manager, G.H. Blackburn, had been in the trade since 1902, having previously been a lanternist who once assisted Sir Ernest Shackleton during lectures. There was a full programme for the opening of the New Palace: Miss Abigail Dobbs sang the National Anthem, accompanied by the twelve-piece orchestra and conducted by Corbet Sheldon, the film was *Quinneys* and Dr Tootell played the organ.

The New Palace survived the Blitz and in 1952 was given a more modern name, the Gaumont. In the 1960s, Beatlemania arrived as the Beatles films *A Hard Day's Night* and *Help* were shown. The Gaumont finally closed in 1980 and became a nightclub. Only its listed frontage saved it from demolition.

*An advertisement for* The Drag Net *at the New Palace.*

Top: *A Livermore's Palace letterhead, 1912.*

Above: *The People's Palace orchestra, 1912.*

Below: *Musical Conductor Frederic Fey's letterhead, 1912.*

*Known over the years as Livermore's Palace, the People's Palace and the New Palace, most people will remember the cinema as the Gaumont.*

# Picturedrome, East Street, Bedminster, c. 1911-1919

The Picturedrome was situated between the Wills cigarette factory and the library on one side and the police station on the other. It is thought that the owners were Mr and Mrs Price. The cinema was known locally as the 'penny pops' because it was 1d to sit at the front and 2d at the back.
In 1912, the Picturedrome was altered by a local builder. By taking in the stables and yard at the back and adding a small projection room, the number of seats was doubled to 450. Before these alterations, it must have been just a small hall, with a projector standing between rows of benches – a basic penny gaff.

The Picturedrome had some competition from nearby Bedminster Town Hall, which opened in 1909. Survival became more difficult once the Bedminster Hippodrome turned to cinema in 1915. The Picturedrome closed its doors in 1919 and became the Dockers' Hall.

*The Bedminster Picturedrome.*

# Premier, Gloucester Road, 1914-1963

The Premier was built by Samuel Justin, a locally born engineer who owned a bicycle business in Stokes Croft and also ran a seaside amusement arcade on Birnbeck Island at Weston-super-Mare. There he saw a bioscope show and was bitten by the cinema bug. The Premier was situated on Gloucester Road, between Dongola Avenue and Ashley Down Road.

In the days of silent films, the Premier added their own sound effects. For *The Four Horsemen of the Apocalypse*, they used indoor fireworks but things didn't go to plan and they were almost choked by the smoke. Chains dragged backstage were used for *Ben Hur* and *The Hunchback of Notre Dame*.

The picture house was renovated in the 1920s. It had 600 seats downstairs and 100 in the balcony. Samuel Justin took over the Premier and the Olympia and ran both cinemas very successfully. In later years, the Premier was owned by Oliver Pugsley. It closed in 1964, the last film being *The Defiant Ones*, starring Tony Curtis and Sidney Poitier.

The new owners were builder's merchants A.E. Alders, who already had premises at Nos 361-363 and No. 335 Gloucester Road. They paid the Pugsleys £25,000 for the site. The building was kept much as it was, with just the seats being removed. The foyer became the paint shop, wallpaper was displayed and sold in the balcony, the projection room was used as the storeroom and the auditorium was used for bathrooms and central heating. It is now a supermarket.

---

## Premier Cinema Theatre
### GLOUCESTER ROAD.

Showing FRIDAY, AUG. 14th, & SATURDAY, AUG. 15th, only

# ENGLAND'S FIRST LINE OF DEFENCE

GRAND NAVAL SPECTACLE !!

THE BRITISH FLEET
Including
H.M.S. "BRISTOL," "BIRMINGHAM," "HIBERNIA," &c.
SUBMARINES, HYDROPLANE FLIGHTS, &c.

NO ADVANCE IN PRICES

---

# PREMIER
### CINEMA THEATRE,
Gloucester Road, BRISTOL.

Continuous Performance 3 to 10.30

Week commencing MONDAY, OCTOBER 5th, 1914

Monday, Tuesday, Wednesday,

## Honour Redeemed
An Exciting Drama of Fighting and the storming of an Arab Fort.

### The Vengeance of the Vacquero
Sensational Kalem Drama.

LATEST WAR PICTURES

Thursday, Friday, Saturday,

# DANGERS OF THE VELDT
A Thrilling Bison Drama of Wild Life in Africa.

### Night Riders of Petersham
Great Vitagraph Feature full of Novel Sensations.

Longest Programme in Bristol.

Prices   -   3d., 4d., 6d., 9d.

*Programmes advertising forthcoming attractions at the Premier.*

## Pringle's Picture Palace/Zetland/Scala, Cromwell Road, St Andrews, 1910-1974

This cinema was situated where Gloucester Road meets Cheltenham Road, close to North Street. The GWR and LMS railways had an agency booking office nearby. The cinema was designed by W.H. Watkins and owned by Ralph Pringle, hence its name Pringle's Picture Palace. Three shops and two houses were demolished before building could start. It opened in 1910 and was better than the penny gaffs of the time, as it had a furnished lounge and a grand circle which was reached by way of a marble staircase. It seated 1,000 downstairs and 400 in the circle. At one time, it also had a Wurlitzer organ. This was one of the cinemas that Cary Grant visited as a child, to watch his favourite slapstick comedy films (*see* also the Clare Street Picture House and the Metropole).

In 1914, it was sold to the same company who owned the Cheltenham Road cinema and its name changed to the Zetland. In 1933, it was sold again, this time to Harris Cinemas Ltd, and later became known as the Scala. It closed in 1974, despite a 2,000-name petition, and became a furniture store. It was later demolished to make way for flats.

## Queen's Picture House, No. 17 Peter Street, 1910-1933

The Queen's was Bristol's first purpose-built cinema. Situated in Peter Street, which was in the Castle Street area, it was owned by British Electric Theatres, a small company from the Home Counties. The company also took over the King's cinema for a short time. In 1915, the Queen's was taken over by the Pugsley family. This was their second cinema; the Globe was the first.

The coat of arms of the city of Bristol stood proudly over the rather wide entrance of the Queen's. An unusual feature of the cinema was its sliding roof, a 16ft by 12ft section of the roof that could be moved aside to let the fresh air in and the smoke out. The staff always claimed that if it rained they could operate the winch so quickly that no one got wet.

The cinema seated 380. There were 45 seats at 1s 3d, 75 at 1s, 101 at 9d and 159 at 6d. It was one of the last picture houses to move over to talkies. Cyril Ashford was one of the musicians at the Queen's, playing the violin. When talkies came in and he no longer had a job, Oliver Pugsley made him manager at the Globe.

In 1933, the Queen's was closed and demolished and the News Theatre was built on the site.

Opposite top: *The Premier in its last days as a cinema.*

Opposite below left: *The Scala.*

Opposite below right: *The Queen's Picture House.*

Above: *The interior of the Queen's, with its sliding roof which let the smoke out and the fresh air in.*

Left: *Oliver Pugsley, owner of the Queen's.*

# Redcliffe Hall Picture Palace, Redcliffe Hill, 1911–1941

Redcliffe Hall Picture Palace was situated on Redcliffe Hill, opposite Guinea Street, and could seat about 100. In 1919, the owner was E.F. Harris. In 1940, it was Harold A. Tweed.

It was considered to be one of Bristol's worst fleapits and even had a problem with rats. A local resident described it as 'a big dreary, dark place. It seemed to have a lot of big posts, you had to be careful not to sit behind one or you couldn't see the picture. It was good value if you didn't mind seeing older films after other cinemas had had them.'

Fleas were a problem in some cinemas and the staff had to deal with them. A slide would appear on the screen during the interval, showing a lady in a crinoline surrounded by flowers. It was announced that the cinema would now be sprayed with 'June' perfume. Then the usherettes would walk up the aisle with a flit gun, spraying left, right and centre. Those seated near the gangways would be covered in the stuff. When that slide appeared on screen, the men would all head for the toilets, not wanting to smell of 'June'!

In 1941, the Redcliffe Hall Picture Palace was completely destroyed during the Blitz.

*Redcliffe Hall Picture Palace.*

# Regent, Castle Street, 1928-1940

The Regent opened on Monday 30 July 1928. The manager was E.A. Barry. It was described as a place of high entertainment, not just a cinema. There was a troupe of nine girls known as the Regent Girls, inseparable dancers called Graham and Douglas, and soprano singer Mademoiselle Rita Colere, supported by a twenty-two-piece orchestra. There was also a Wurlitzer organ which rose from beneath the stage. The organist was Frank Matthews.

The main entrance in Castle Street opened into a spacious crush hall, which eliminated queues outside and allowed 1,000 people to wait in comfort and under cover. The decoration was of a mainly Roman design and the colour scheme was ivory and Titian reds, purples and gold. The hall contained a wide staircase, giving easy access to the tea lounge and auditorium. The tea lounge was 120ft long. Tea was served on a dainty tray and could be consumed while watching the film. The auditorium had 2,014 seats plus standing room for another 212 at the back of the stalls. The entrance to the stalls was in Peter Street and had its own crush hall. The floor area of the stage itself was approximately 2,000ft. The cinema also had changing rooms for the variety acts. Patrons often arrived in evening dress and the usherettes wore red dresses, which matched the seats and décor, with brass buttons. They were inspected daily and buttons and shoes had to shine.

The Regent was designed by W.H. Watkins and was built to replace the Clare Street Picture House. It took two years to build. The first film shown was *The Magic Flame* and the cinema received telegrams from the film's stars, Ronald Coleman and Vilma Banky. Bristol film star Jessie Matthews once made an appearance there. The first talkie to be screened at the Regent was *The Donovan Affair*.

On 24 November 1940, Castle Street was bombed. Luckily, it was a Sunday so the Regent was empty. If the bombing had occurred a week later, the cinema would have been full as the ban on Sunday opening was about to be lifted. The building was gutted but not totally destroyed. Its owners were keen to rebuild but materials were difficult to obtain and the city council weren't sure about the future of the Castle Street site. Its sad shell remained until the end of the 1950s, when the site became a car park. It is now part of Castle Park.

*An advertisement for the Regent.*

Right: *The Regent in Castle Street.*

Below: *The auditorium.*

*The ornate interior of the Regent in Castle Street.*

Left: *A Loxton sketch of the Regent, Kingswood.*

Opposite above: *An advertisement for the Regent, Kingswood.*

Opposite below: *The Regent, Kingswood.*

# Regent picture house, Regent Street, Kingswood, 1912-1949

The Kingswood Regent opened in 1912. Mr Moon was the owner and Mr Kear the manager. It was a basic building with benches, and there was a piano at the front to accompany the silent films. There was always a 2d rush on Saturday afternoons, when there was a programme of cartoons for children. Winkles, eaten from their shells with a pin, and peanuts, also in their shells, were the regular treats for people at the Regent. If the film was below par, the shells would be thrown at the screen. The cinema closed in 1949 and a Be Wise store now stands on the site.

## Regent Picture House

REGENT ST., KINGSWOOD, BRISTOL

*Continuous Performances Nightly From 6.30. Children's Matinee Saturday at 2. Evening 5.30 to 10.30.*

VISIT THE REGENT PICTURE HOUSE
THE KINEMA THAT ALWAYS GIVES FULL VALUE

The Picture House, Kingswood, Bristol

# Rex, North Street, Bedminster, 1940-1980

The Rex opened on 9 December 1940 with the film *Rebecca*, based on the novel by Daphne du Maurier, starring Laurence Olivier and Joan Fontaine. The opening was low-key compared to the usual ABC cinema opening events but it was wartime.

The Rex was hit during the Blitz of Good Friday 1941. The heart of the cinema was torn out and although the four walls were left standing, the seats were blasted out onto the rooftops of neighbouring houses. They had only been open for about four months and that was how long they were closed for rebuilding.

In January 1946, a new manager, Mr Eric G. Handford, arrived and he certainly put this ABC cinema on the map. He was awarded the title of National Showman of the Year in 1951/52, 1956/57 and 1958/59. Handford was born in Bristol, educated at Bristol Cathedral School and began his career in Birmingham with the ABC group, where he soon became assistant manager. During the Second World War, he joined the Royal Navy but he resumed his cinema career after the war when he joined the Rex. He immediately began to get the cinema involved with the local business community by using advance advertising display boards in the foyer and tying films to local products. He matched local fashion shops with Hollywood glamour by allowing them to display clothes appropriate to the films showing in the cinema. When *Anchors Aweigh*, starring Frank Sinatra, Gene Kelly and Kathryn Grayson, was showing at the Rex, Campbell's Steamers sponsored the display and advertised their day trips. When *Dunkirk* was screened, Eric Handford organised a telephone link between his cinema and one in Dunkirk, France, which was also called the Rex. He also contacted Bristol, Connecticut and set up an Anglo-American friendship scheme in connection with the film *The Miniver Story*. The foyer was also used for charitable purposes, such as carol services to raise money for the St Francis Youth Club and toy collections for Frenchay, Winford and Ham Green Hospitals.

It has always been the policy of the ABC group to bring the stars of the films showing in their cinemas around the country to do promotions. Van Johnson, Bryan Forbes and Jess Conrad all came to the Rex in the 1960s. Pamela Franklin and Michelle Dotrice – who went on to play Betty in the TV programme *Some Mothers Do 'Av 'Em* – came to promote *And Soon the Darkness*. To celebrate the twenty-first anniversary of the opening of the Rex, the cinema showed *What a Whopper!*, starring Adam Faith, and his co-star Marie French attended the event.

The cinema closed in August 1980; the last film shown was *Superman*. The lessee for the last two years was Bernard Snowball. Like most local cinemas, the Rex became a bingo hall. To give its new owners credit, the interior has been restored with great integrity. A short film called *Happiness is a Full House* was made there in 1998 and the premiere was held in the old Rex.

Opposite above: *The Rex showed* What a Whopper! *to celebrate its twenty-first anniversary.*

Opposite below: *The interior of the Rex.*

*The staff gather on the steps leading to the circle and stalls to celebrate the Rex's twenty-fifth anniversary in 1965. Actor Jess Conrad was the guest of honour.*

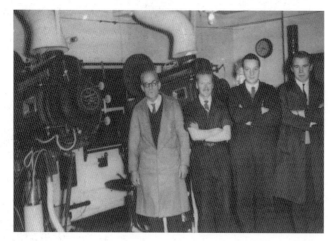

*A rare picture of the projection room. From left to right: Stan Nash, Len Gamlin, Mr Ford and Mr Bailey. Stan Nash worked in many of Bristol's cinemas.*

*Staff from the Rex in the 1960s.*

# "REX"

## CINÉMA - MUSIC HALL

### 21, RUE DAVID D'ANGERS - DUNKERQUE

**TÉLÉPHONE 24.83**

S.A.R.L. - SAINTE CECILE AU CAPITAL DE 8.000.000 FRS

*Dunkerque, le* 27 JUIN 1956

Above: *A letterhead from the Rex cinema in Dunkerque.*

Right: *A toy collection at the Rex for the children's hospital.*

*The Rex during its time as the Club Granada bingo hall.*

*Today, the Rex is a Gala bingo hall.*

# Ritz, Bristol Hill, Brislington, 1938-1968

The Ritz cinema stood on Bristol Hill, on the corner of Warrington Road. It opened on Saturday 8 October 1938 and was advertised at the time as 'the showpiece of the west'. The *Bristol Evening Post* devoted a whole page to its opening. The cinema was built on a piece of grassland where an oak tree had been planted in 1863 to commemorate the marriage of the Prince of Wales (later King Edward VII), so the builders had to be very careful. It was designed by W.H. Watkins and built by Hyatt and Neate of Westbury-on-Trym, and took six months to build. The structure had a reinforced-concrete frame filled in with panels of brickwork. The outside was painted cream, with green-glazed roof tiles. Inside, there was comfy green and black seating for 1,400 people, a scented ventilation system and facilities for the deaf.

The first film to be shown at the Ritz was *A Yank in Oxford*, starring Robert Taylor, and the queues stretched all the way down Bristol Hill. Cockney actor Wally Patch, who starred in over 100 films, opened the cinema and commented that 'it does credit to everyone concerned and is as good a place as people go anywhere in England'. The Lord Mayor, Alderman John James Milton, and his wife also gave the cinema their blessing.

The Ritz survived the Second World War without damage. Its roof was camouflaged and the staff kept the bombs off the roof by keeping watch, sand buckets at the ready. It was used for live big band shows for the American troops stationed in Brislington. It was also on standby to be converted into a hospital if necessary, but luckily it wasn't needed.

After the war, the cinema somehow managed to survive. However, cinemas were slowly going out of fashion and the Ritz was no exception. That didn't stop celebrities visiting over the years. Richard Pasco, Norman Wisdom and Winifred Atwell all came to the Ritz, as did the singers Pearl Carr and Teddy Johnson, who came to see the film *The Dangerous Years* with Frankie Vaughan. The last film was shown there on 20 July 1968. In 1970, the building was partially demolished and became a Kwik Save supermarket; it is now a DIY store. Only the rear of the original building survives.

Left: *The Ritz*.

Below: *An advertisement for* Jamaica Inn *and* Star Reporter *at the Ritz.*

**THE RITZ** Tel. 768131

CINEMA, BRISLINGTON.
TO-DAY ----- Continuous from 2.0.
CHARLES LAUGHTON in
**"JAMAICA INN"**
(A) At 2.15 · 5.30 · 8.50
Also ALAN BAXTER in
**"STAR REPORTER"**
A· At 4.15 and 7.30

# St George's Hall/Granada, Church Road, Redfield, 1912-1961

The official name of this cinema was the St George's Hall Electric Palace. When it first opened in 1912, the entrance was situated in Victoria Road (now Victoria Parade). There was no permanent sign outside, just a board that was put out when the cinema was open. The manager was Tommy Simmonds, the projectionist was Eldrey Carey and there was one ticket girl and a pianist. The benches inside were often pushed closer together to make room for more people if the film was popular.

By the late 1920s, the Pugsley family had taken over this tiny cinema. As well as the cinema (which had previously been a slaughterhouse), they purchased the building next door, which had been a coffin storeroom owned by Osbourne's undertakers downstairs and the Victoria Road Mission upstairs. They also bought several nearby shops. The Pugsleys joined all these premises together to make a larger cinema and moved the entrance to a more prominent position on Church Road. The foyer was long and was a great place to queue if it rained.

The cinema opened with the slightly shorter name of St George's Hall on 26 December 1927. They showed two of the biggest films of the day, *Don Juan* and *Big Parade*. There was an orchestra consisting of two violinists, a drummer, a trumpeter, a cellist and a bassist. The cinema seated 750. Downstairs there were 168 seats at 9d each and 237 seats at 6d. Upstairs were 43 seats at 1s 6d, 176 seats at 1s 3d and 126 seats at 1s. There were two ticket offices, one in Church Road and one in Victoria Parade for the 6d rush. The first day's takings were £52 13s 1d. The films were shown for six days and the total takings for the first week were £254 19s 2d.

The projectionist at this time was Jack Wyard and the film boy was Ernest Davies, both of whom were future managers of the Globe cinema. The manager of St George's Hall was J.A. Wilson, a staunch Catholic with strong views: there was no funny business like courting and cuddling inside his cinema! There was an ice-cream salesgirl, who was paid on commission; later the usherettes took over this job. The girls worked hard at this cinema, as there were lots of stairs to climb to reach the seats.

By the end of 1929, St George's Hall had been renamed the Granada and the talkies had arrived. All the musicians lost their jobs with no redundancy pay. The cinema survived the Second World War undamaged but things went downhill after the war and the cinema closed in 1961. The last film shown was *The Alamo*, starring John Wayne.

The building became a bingo hall called the Granada Social Club, under new ownership. The screen and chairs downstairs disappeared but upstairs remained the same. When it was a cinema, those sitting upstairs could leave by way of the fire escape and that was also the only way into the projection box. The fire escape was demolished when the cinema became a bingo hall and the projection box with all its equipment was sealed shut.

The bingo hall was run for many years by Eastbourne Bingo, launched by Bill O'Mahony in the 1960s and continued by his sons Mike and Dermot. It was a very friendly place where everyone knew each other but it could not compete when a brand new bingo hall opened in Barton Hill in the 1990s. Wetherspoon's bought the site and turned it into a pub, spending nearly £1 million on renovations. It opened on 8 December 1998 as St George's Hall, its old cinema name. The old auditorium is used as a kitchen and storage area and customers drink in the old foyer.

Opposite: *A drawing of the Granada by Dennis Stephenson, 1998.*

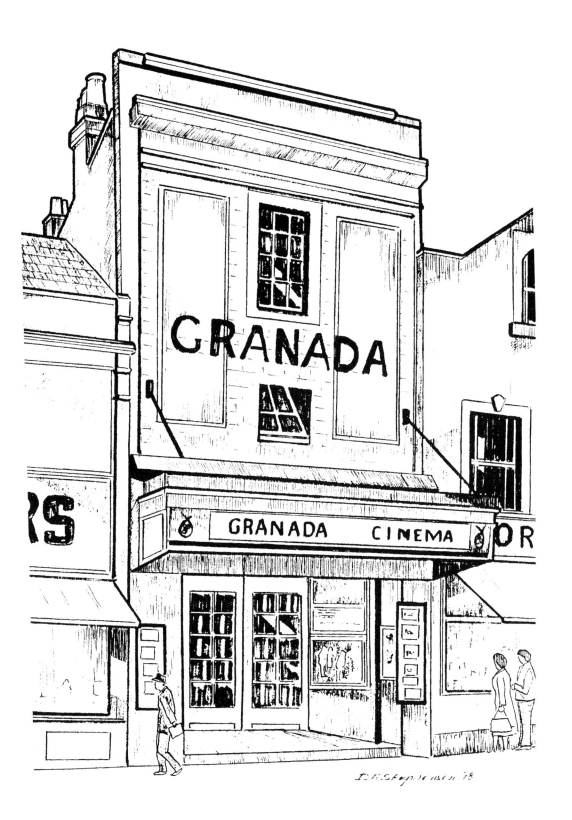

GRANADA

GRANADA CINEMA

D.A.Stephenson '78

*The interior of the Granada, seen from the stage.*

*The Granada's screen, hidden behind heavy curtains.*

*The City Trumpeter Bill Cozens, seen here on the left with Arthur Golding outside the Lord Mayor's Chapel, played for many years at St George's Hall, the Park and the Empire. Born in 1898, he was a self-taught musician and played with many orchestras, even performing for royalty.*

*The Granada Social Club in the 1960s.*

# Savoy, Station Road, Shirehampton, 1933-1962

The Savoy opened in 1933. It was owned by Emmanuel Harris and designed by prolific Bristol cinema designer W.H. Watkins, with 700 seats downstairs and 200 in the balcony. Its customers came from Shirehampton, Sea Mills, Kingsweston and Henbury. People even came across from Pill, using the local ferry boat. The cinema was known locally as the Cabbage, after Savoy cabbage.

In 1962, the Savoy closed, its last film being *Carry On Cruising*. Its Welsh owners converted it into a bingo hall, which was more profitable. It was later bought by Rank Cinemas and finally closed in June 2000. There were plans to turn the building into a supermarket but local traders opposed them. It remained empty and was finally demolished in 2003 to make way for thirty-eight new apartments.

*The Savoy after it had been converted into a bingo hall.*

*An advertisement for the Savoy.*

# Staple Hill Picture House/Regal, 1912-1963

In 1905, Frank Wren, a builder who lived at The Limes in Downend, purchased the land on which the cinema stands. The cinema, known as the Staple Hill Picture House, was built in 1912. In 1913, Wren leased the land to his son, Herbert F. Wren. By 1914, Frank had died and Herbert had purchased the nearby Clematis House (now called Riebeck House) and Bank House, built around 1847. In 1927, the cinema was extended and much altered. Bank House was incorporated into the building, as was the old gospel hall, built around 1900, that stood behind. A dome was removed from the roof and the area beneath became a café. The cinema, now called the Regal, reopened on Monday 29 August 1927 with the silent film *Mademoiselle From Armentieres*.

In 1940, Herbert sold the cinema to his son and daughter. The family had always lived next door to the picture house and there was a linking door that allowed access to and from the buildings. There were also two National Gas Engines at the bottom of the garden, one big and one small, allowing them to generate their own electricity. The cinema closed in late November 1963, its last films being *Psycho* and *The Blob*. It was then sold to a new company, who converted it into a more profitable and popular bingo hall. It closed in 1992, unable to compete with a new purpose-built Bingo Palace that had opened in Fishponds. The building stood empty for at least seven years. Plans were put forward and rejected and local people were worried that this landmark would be vandalised or disappear completely. It is now a place of worship known as the Sanctuary church.

*A sketch of the Regal by S. Loxton.*

## REGAL CINEMA

For your Entertainment

We present
Attractive Programmes
Under Ideal Conditions
All the latest Equipment
DAILY from 5-20 p.m.
SATURDAYS 4-15 p.m.
Matinees:
MONDAY WEDNESDAY
& THURSDAY AT 1-45 p.m.

**CHILDREN'S MATINEE
SATURDAY at 1 p.m.**

**Free Car Park for over 100 Cars**

Popular Prices       Phone 53534

Above: *The Regal in 1927.*

Left: *An 1946 advertisement for the Regal.*

Below: *The Regal became the Mayfair Bingo &
Social Club.*

# Studios One to Four, The Pithay, 1973–1986

When the studios opened in 1973, they were believed to be the future of cinema: small studios in one building, all showing different films but using just one set of staff. This saved a great deal of money for the owners, who had a further set of studios, Five to Seven, at Henleaze. The studios were so small that the staff often referred to them as 'rabbit hutches'. Before Studios One to Four opened, the Magnet Bowling Alley used to stand on this site. The cinema closed in 1986 and became a nightclub.

# Tivoli, Broadmead, c. 1912–1916

The Tivoli was a very small cinema, seating only 300, and it always struggled to compete with the larger cinemas. It used to be a music hall and was known as the Star Music Hall until around 1896. It was owned by a real showman, Mr E. 'Teddy' Leon, who was described as 'a smart gentleman who usually wore a frock coat and a very shiny box hat'. He also owned the Empire in Old Market and ran nine dentistry businesses in South Wales and the West. He had been a stage performer by the name of Edward Aubrey Goodman and had over twenty-five years' experience in the business. The Tivoli and the Empire ran programmes jointly: the artists would finish their act in one theatre and rush off to the next, still in full make-up.

  The Tivoli was probably one of the first theatres in Bristol to show moving pictures; they were first shown there in 1896, although only for a few weeks as films were considered at the time to be just another novelty act. The Tivoli became a cinema around 1912, with a grand reopening that included performances on screen and off by 'Montana Joe', a world-famous cowboy actor, who gave three lectures a day dressed in full cowboy gear. The cinema only survived for four years. The building was demolished in 1952.

*The Tivoli.*

# Town Hall, Cannon Street, Bedminster, 1909-1954

Ralph Pringle took out a lease on the old Town Hall in Bedminster in April 1909. The building, situated two doors away from the London Inn, dates back to 1892 and it was there that Clara Butt gave her first public performance. Pringle converted it into a very basic cinema, just a hall with rows of seats and a projector. The music was provided by a single piano. The staff were offered commission of 1s if they sold £1 worth of chocolate, which was a lot of chocolate.

By 1915, F.J. Price was the owner. He sold it to Bruce Atkinson, who owned or leased many cinemas in the area. In later years, the building became run-down and the roof leaked badly. Patrons had to know where to sit to avoid the leaks; many used an umbrella. The cinema closed in 1954 and became a supermarket and then a furniture store. The building still stands today; it no longer looks like a cinema from the outside but inside it is possible to see where the screen once was.

# Triangle, Clifton, 1914-1940

The Triangle cinema was owned by Emmanuel Harris, who came to Bristol in 1910. He converted the Triangle Hall in Clifton into a roller-skating rink, having already opened a rink in Rupert Street. When skating declined in popularity, Harris turned the hall into a cinema showing silent films. It opened in 1914.

Harris employed the best designer in W.H. Watkins and added a balcony and wide, comfortable seats. The cinema had a pillared entrance that curved around the corner. There was a splendid café in which customers could see the screen while seated at the tables. There was also a superb orchestra, conducted by Clifton music master Maurice Alexander. A trio and pianist filled in between showings. The Triangle was a very popular place and Harris would often walk down the aisle of the auditorium and ask the patrons who had seen the round to kindly leave to make room for the large queue outside.

Members of the Fry and Cadbury families often arrived in their limousines to see a film. Conrad Fry, who could have bought the entire cinema, loved to race to get a ticket for the 6d matinee. He would then tip the commissionaire half a crown on his way out.

In 1921, the Whiteladies cinema opened. Harris saw this as a threat, as it was very close to his premises and offered films of the same quality as those shown at the Triangle. He responded by tying the Triangle to a nine-month contract with MGM, 20th Century Fox, First National and Universal, which allowed him to get the pick of their best films and stole the Whiteladies cinema's thunder.

Harris later gained control of the Whiteladies. In the 1930s, he suddenly sold the Triangle and the Whiteladies to the ABC group, along with another cinema he owned in Bath, the Beau Nash, for a staggering £250,000. He later bought the Scala, the Plaza and a cinema in Chippenham, leased the Baths on Gloucester Road and built the Savoy at Shirehampton. The Triangle continued to do well under the ABC group but was destroyed by enemy bombing on 24 November 1940.

*Children queueing up for the Jackie Coogan film* Trouble *at the Bedminster Town Hall.*

*The pillared entrance of the Triangle, which had stained-glass panels around the canopy displaying the cinema's name.*

Left: *The Triangle after it had
been taken over by ABC.*

Below: *An advertisement for
films at the Triangle.*

MON. TUES.
& WEDNESDAY.
CLIFTON

# TRIANGLE

DAILY-
2 TO 10·30.
CLIFTON

MAY McAVOY and
LIONEL BARRYMORE in "THE LION AND THE MOUSE,"
A Powerful Drama of Modern Life.          At 3.40, 6.25, 9.15.          Also
Louise Fazenda in "PAY AS YOU ENTER,"
The Fastest Joy Ride of the Season.          At 2.15, 5.5, 7.55.

# Vandyck, Nos 748-756 Fishponds Road, 1926-1973

The Vandyck was designed by W.H. Watkins and owned by the Vandyck Picture Co. The company's chairman was S. Gamlin, who built the Cabot and owned the Park. The cinema seated 742 in the stalls and 332 upstairs in a large balcony, and had a full orchestra. The first manager was George Harris.

Advertised as 'the city cinema in the suburbs', the Vandyck was opened by the Lord Mayor, Alderman Frank Moore, at 7.30 p.m. on 5 November 1926. An orchestra was hired from Cardiff and there were performances from comedian John Henry and soprano Mavis Bennett. The money from the evening went to the Lord Mayor's Christmas Fund and the Wireless for Hospitals Fund. The Vandyck officially opened on the day after the concert, Saturday 6 November, showing *The Enduring Flame*, starring William Boyd and Vera Reynolds, and *Nancy From Nowhere*, starring Bebe Daniels.

*That'll be the Day*, starring David Essex and Ringo Starr, was the last film shown at the Vandyck before it closed in 1973. After a £100,000 facelift, it became a bingo hall, despite a petition signed by several thousand people. The owners pointed out that 'the local people can't complain because they didn't support it when it was a cinema. It has been 80 per cent empty over the past year'. The bingo hall closed in 1996 after the new, purpose-built Riva bingo hall opened nearby. Wetherspoon's spent £1.2 million to convert it into a pub called the Vandyck Forum.

*The Vandyck.*

**THE VANDYCK**
PICTURE HOUSE
FISHPONDS

TO-NIGHT,
TUESDAY and WEDNESDAY.

ON THE SCREEN:—
**SAMMY COHEN**
in a Riot of Laughter,
**"PLASTERED IN PARIS."**
Also:—
LUPINO LANE in
**"FANDANGO."**

ON THE STAGE:—
**CARO & PARTNER**
Up in the air with a Personality.

Right: *An advertisement for the Vandyck.*

Below: *The Vandyck Forum pub, 2005.*

# Vestry Hall, Pennywell Road, 1909-1954

The Vestry Hall was one of Ralph Pringle's cinemas. A Quaker workhouse, erected on land owned by Maj. Nathaniel Wade, stood on this site from 1696. It was built to relieve the poor people of this district and was later rebuilt as it couldn't cope with the demand. The hall was built in 1880 as a segregated sports and activities gymnasium owned by the Bristol Corporation Baths Department. When Pringle took over the building, it became a real penny gaff, with rows of seats and a lick of paint. For the very poor people of that district, it was magical. It was situated in a very densely populated area and served the people of Old Market, The Dings, St Jude's and Easton. It could seat 520 people and had a small stage, about 20 feet square. The screen was situated above the stage and the music was supplied by a single piano player. Local residents recall that:

> there were forms in the front and seats at the back. You could sit anywhere for 3d, which was a lot of money for most of those people but everyone wanted to see the moving pictures. Even the fumes from the arc lights didn't bother us. The walls were soon yellow from carbon dust and the seats needed frequent fumigation. We called it the bughouse. If you didn't have them when you went in, you probably had them by the time you came out!

When Ralph Pringle left Bristol, Bruce Atkinson – who had worked for Ralph in earlier years – took over the Vestry Hall. Even as late as 1922, there was just one person employed to take the tickets, carry the heavy spools of film up to the manager's office and then rewind them ready for the next show.

The Vestry Hall closed in 1954, when much of the area that it served was bulldozed. The building has had numerous owners since and is still standing.

*Local children pose for the camera before seeing a film at the Vestry Hall.*

*The Vestry Hall.*

*The building still stands today, 125 years after it was built.*

# Victoria Rooms/Clifton Cinema, Queens Road, Clifton, *c.* 1919-1922

Around 1919, the Victoria Rooms were leased from Bristol University and became the Clifton cinema. However, there were continuous problems over its licence (and the large name plate that stood outside) and the building was only used as a cinema for just over two years. The building still stands majestically, as it first did, to this day.

*The Victoria Rooms became the Clifton cinema for just over two years.*

*An advertisement for* Levante *at the Victoria Rooms.*

# Whiteladies Picture House, Whiteladies Road, Clifton, 1921-2002

The Whiteladies Picture House opened on 29 November 1921. The first film shown was *Pollyanna*, starring Mary Pickford. The opening was a very grand affair and all 1,300 seats were filled. A number of dignitaries were present, notably Her Grace the Duchess of Beaufort, the Archdeacon of Bristol, Col. Paul Bush, Revd D.H. Arnold Thomas, Col. H.G. Woodcock and Alderman J. Boyd. The cinema achieved instant respectability.

The cinema was designed by James Henry La Trobe and Thomas Henry Weston. They retained part of the nunnery that used to stand on the site, whose white-robed nuns probably gave Whiteladies Road its name. The entrance hall featured columns of marble from Italy and had a mosaic floor described as 'marble crazy'. While waiting for the film, patrons could relax in the foyer or the luxurious Rendezvous Café. Inside the auditorium were eight murals that combined artistic feeling with a sense of humour. They included 'The Pied Piper of Hamelin', 'The First Voyage of Sinbad the Sailor', 'Ali Baba in the Robbers' Cave', 'The Magic Carpet', 'The Greeks Setting Out to Rescue Helen from the Trojans', 'Alice in Wonderland' and 'The New Marriage of Omar Khayam'. The building had a tower with the cinema's name set into the concrete at the top. Electric light was used to illuminate both the inside and outside of the cinema.

The chairman, Mr Albert Moon (*see* the Gem and the Regent, Kingswood) looked upon the cinema as a public institution for the welfare, benefit, elevation and amusement of the people and promised to encourage British art and, where possible, book films produced by British companies. The first manager was Norman Robertson, who had come from the Clare Street Picture House.

The Whiteladies Picture House had a bitter rivalry with the Triangle, owned by Emmanuel Harris, as both cinemas were chasing the same high-class Clifton patrons. Mr Harris later took over the Whiteladies, before it was sold to the ABC group. The cinema was very slow to move over to the talkies and even advertised itself as 'the home of the silent screen'. However, the supply of silent films eventually dried up and they had to install a sound system.

The Whiteladies hosted the local premiere of *Oklahoma* in 1955 and of *Gigi* in 1958. ABC staged these events with some flair and they generated good publicity. In 1961, Richard Todd visited the cinema to promote *Don't Bother to Knock*, and the stars of *Some People*, Kenneth Moore and Ray Brookes, came to promote the Bristol-made film in 1962. When the John Wayne film *The Green Berets* was showing, audiences were greeted by protesters with placards when they left the cinema, which was somewhat intimidating. Many people considered the film to be propaganda for the Vietnam War and there were protests around the country.

In 1978, the Whiteladies was converted into three mini screens and was threatened with closure on several occasions. It finally closed in 2002. Protests came in thick and fast and the campaign to save the cinema had the backing of celebrities such as Tony Robinson, Paul McGann and Nick Park – the man who gave us Wallace and Gromit – to name but a few. The campaign is still on-going, but the cinema remains closed. The building still stands in Whiteladies Road.

Opposite above: *The Whiteladies Picture House in its prime.*

Opposite below: *An unusual advertisement for the Whiteladies, restored for this book by Bristol historian John Penny.*

Luxurious
Cafe
Restaurant
Open
Daily.

Luxurious
Cafe
Restaurant
Open
Daily.

# White Ladies Picture House

Opens to the Public on <u>TUESDAY NEXT</u> at 6.30 p.m., and will, from 2.30 to 10 p.m. daily during the week, present the charming and vivacious

## MARY PICKFORD
## in her Great Success: "POLLYANNA"

Also an Interesting and Varied Programme, including (for the first of a series), the new PRIZMA COLOUR FILMS

PRICES OF ADMISSION                    2/-. 1/6. 1/- and 9d.
BOOKS OF TICKETS WITH LIBERAL DISCOUNT CAN BE OBTAINED FROM THE MANAGER.

## "THE RENDEZVOUS"

THIS LUXURIOUS CAFE OPEN DAILY for LUNCHEONS, TEAS, DINNERS and SUPPERS—10 a.m. to 10 p.m.
Orchestra under the direction of MR. W. E. FOWLER, L.R.A.M., A.R.C.M.
Manager: MR. NORMAN ROBERTSON
(late of The Picture House, Clare Street).

*The interior of the Whiteladies.*

*The Whiteladies Picture House.*

Opposite above: *The ABC managers gather in the Dick Turpin bar next to the Whiteladies on the occasion of Tom Purdie's retirement in September 1967. Ron White, in the centre, was the Regional Manager.*

Right: *An advertisement for
the Whiteladies.*

MON., TUES.
& WEDNESDAY.
CLIFTON
**WHITELADIES**
DAILY
2 - TO 10·30
CLIFTON
FIRST PRESENTATION IN BRISTOL.
**Claire Windsor** in **"THE MODERN FLAPPER,"**
An Eyeful of Delightful Entertainment.     At 2.0, 4.50, 7.40.     Also
**Ramon Novarro and Alice Terry** in **"SCARAMOUCHE,"**
The Miracle of the Silent Screen.     At 3.10, 6.0, 8.50.

*The Whiteladies, 1998.*

# ENDPIECE

*Bristol cinema owners – a potted history:*

**ABC** was started by a Scotsman called John Maxwell in 1928. The company bought existing buildings and rented and built others. In Bristol, Maxwell leased or owned the Whiteladies, the Triangle, the King's, the Cabot, the Empire and the Park.

**George Allen** built His Majesty's, Eastville Hippodrome and the Metropole and, much later, the Ritz and the Carlton. His wife continued to run the business after his death in the late 1950s.

**Andrew Bruce Atkinson** (1886-1948), who was always known as Bruce, was born in Bristol. He started his career as a concert party artist, then worked for Ralph Pringle. He later managed or owned the Zetland, the Dolphin, the Vestry, the Baths, the Redcliffe, Bedminster Town Hall, the Plaza, the Scala, the Kingsway and the Regent, Kingswood. His sons later took over the business.

**Ralph Bromhead** owned the King's and ran the Coliseum before becoming one of the founders of the Gaumont Cinema empire.

**Enrico Carreras** and his son James owned the King's cinema at one time. **James** was later knighted and is remembered for his connection with Hammer films.

**The Chamberlain family. William** (1866-1946) came to Bristol some time before 1919 with his son Fitzroy, known as Roy. He bought the Magnet cinema in 1919 and ran it until it closed in 1937. **Roy** (1892-1973) came to Bristol from Southampton, where he had trained as an electrician, and worked as a part-time projectionist. He leased then bought the Knowle Picture House and built the Gaiety and the Broadway. He became Lord Mayor of Bristol in 1958. **Denys** grew up living next door to the Gaiety as it was being built. He took over the business from his father and sold his last cinema in 1991. Since then, he has given talks and slide shows recalling Bristol cinemas.

**Oscar Deutsch** built the Odeon in Union Street and later took over the Ambassadors in Bedminster and Kingswood, renaming them Odeons. The first two letters of the name Odeon stand for 'Oscar' and 'Deutsch'. He built up a massive chain of cinemas across the country.

**Sidney Thomas Gamlin** (1887-1975) was a Bristol councillor and lived at Stoke Bishop. He had connections with Eastville Chapel and Bristol Rovers football club. He built the Vandyck and the Cabot and later purchased the Park.

**Emmanuel Harris** (d.1948) built the Triangle and took over the Whiteladies, later selling both to the ABC group. He then took over the Zetland (Scala) and Cheltenham Road (Plaza) cinemas. His mother trained with Clara Butt, his uncles were all on the stage and his wife was an excellent cinema pianist. He was the grandfather of 1960s star Anita Harris.

**Samuel Justine** tried his luck in Australia before opening a bicycle business in Stokes Croft and a seaside amusement arcade on Birnbeck Island, Weston-super-Mare, where he first saw moving pictures. He then built the Premier on Gloucester Road and took over the Olympia.

**A.F. Moon** built the Whiteladies and owned the Gem and the Regent, Kingswood. A local politician, he became Lord Mayor of Bristol.

**Ralph Pringle** (1856-1922) formed the North American Animated Picture Co., which toured the country showing films in halls and theatres, including the Colston Hall. He opened his first cinema in 1909, the Bedminster Town Hall, followed by the Dolphin and the Vestry. His best cinema was Pringle's Palace, later called the Scala. In later life, he sold up and left Bristol for Port Talbot, where he ended his days. His body was returned to Bristol for burial and all the big cinema owners attended his funeral.

**The Pugsley family** were very well known and well liked. Representatives of the big film companies, local politicians and staff attended each of their funerals. **Joseph** (1856-1928) started out as a scrap-metal dealer in Cheese Lane and Midland Road, St Philip's, before moving to Lawrence Hill. He went blind before his first cinema, the Globe, was built in 1914. His eldest son, George, was his eyes while the building was taking place. He never saw moving pictures and died just before the talkies arrived. **George** (1879-1954) took over the business from his father, bought the Queen's and rebuilt the St George Picture House. **Oliver** (1890-1957) took over from George while he ran the scrap-metal side of the business. He supervised the building of the Orpheus, injuring himself by falling from the balcony during construction. He was good friends with all of the other cinema owners and they would often all meet up in a local pub – but only if they served draught Bass, Oliver's favourite tipple.

**Oswald Stoll** (d.1942) built the Bristol Hippodrome and then took over the Bedminster Hippodrome. He was later knighted.

**Harry Tomkins** owned the Brislington Picture House from the start and had a film rental business in Victoria Street. His son George eventually took over the business.

**The Wren family. Harry** built and owned the Regal in Staple Hill. **Herbert**, his son, took over the business and then Herbert's children took over from him. The Wrens also owned the Fishponds cinema for a short time.

*The following pages illustrate the strength of community spirit in Bristol's cinemas.*

*Bristol Cinema XI, 1930s. The team played early on a Sunday morning. We know that employees of George Allen and Oliver Pugsley played on the Downs, in Eastville Park and at the old Bristol Rovers ground in Eastville, which is probably where this photograph was taken. Oliver Pugsley is seated on the far right.*

Opposite above: *The Rex Minors, Bedminster. They were runners-up in the Merchant Navy Cup in 1947, losing 2-1. Among the team members are Alan Lancastle, David Hooper, Brian Neale, Derek Johnson, Clifford Johnson and John Raynes.*

Opposite below: *A cricket match between the ABC group and the Odeon group in August 1948, perhaps for charity. The Clifton Suspension Bridge can be seen in the background.*

*The ABC group promote the Rex and the King's cinemas at a local show, c. 1949.*

Opposite above: *Eric Handford, manager of the Rex in Bedminster, allowed local fashion shops to display their clothes in the foyer in connection with the film* Easter Parade.

Opposite below: *Another of Handford's publicity stunts at the Rex, as the Bristol Bulldogs put on a display to coincide with the screening of* Gone With the Wind.

*Film star Van Johnson, who was starring in* The Music Man *at the time, accepted an invitation to a special showing of his film* Kelly and Me, *which he had never actually seen, at the Rex in Bedminster. Pictured with him is manager Eric Handford.*

*Denys Chamberlain, 14 April 2005. He had just given a slideshow and talk about the Gaiety at Knowle Library, which is very close to where the cinema that he owned for so many years once stood. Every seat was full and everyone there knew Mr Chamberlain, who has gone from being a cinema owner to a cinema historian. The library itself will also soon disappear.*

# ZONGAR

THE DARE - DEVIL OF ROMANCE
FEATURING *the* PREMIER STUNT ARTIST

## GEORGE LARKIN

This star has from time to time broken
various limbs no less than seven times in
. carrying out his astounding thrills. .

### IN 5 REELS

To see Larkin rescue the heroine from a motor car, on the brink of a precipice,
as he swoops down in an aeroplane, is only one of the many exciting incidents
in the film which go to make this subject the GREAT public puller which
it undoubtedly is.

RIGHTS FOR WEST OF ENGLAND (INCLUDING
HAMPSHIRE) AND SOUTH WALES OWNED BY

## BRISTOL FILM SERVICE LIMITED,
## 127 VICTORIA STREET, BRISTOL.
GRAMS—"FILMIRE, BRISTOL."                    PHONE—1131 BRISTOL.

*The cover of a publicity brochure for Zongar, one of the silent films sold to local cinemas by Bristol
Film Service Ltd in Victoria Street. The company was owned by the Tomkins family, who also owned the
Brislington Picture Hall.*

# Other local titles published by Tempus

## The Dings and St Philips

DAVE STEPHENSON AND JILL WILLMOTT

This volume provides a glimpse into the history of The Dings and St Philips during the last century. Compiled with over 200 images, this selection highlights some of the changes and events that have taken place in these once industrious Bristol suburbs. Aspects of everyday life are also recalled, from shops, pubs and places of worship to celebrations and local sporting heroes.

0 7524 3556 6

## Kingswood and Two Mile Hill

JILL WILLMOTT

Kingswood and Two Mile Hill was formerly an important coal mining and shoe-manufacturing district and this book highlights the changes and developments to local schools, shops, churches, hospitals, pubs and cinemas (including the Regent Cinema, which opened in 1912), and to the area's industrial scene, including ironmongers, blacksmiths and forges, as well as the larger factories of Douglas Engineering and Langridge's Corset Factory.

0 7524 3311 3

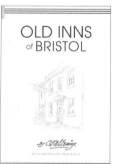

## Old Inns of Bristol

C.F.W. DENING, WITH A NEW PREFACE BY MAURICE FELLS

*Old Inns of Bristol* is a fascinating guide to the historic pubs in the city. First published in 1943, the original book is reproduced here, along with an updated preface by local writer and broadcaster Maurice Fells. This book offers the reader an insight into the life of pubs past and present, from the oddly named Rhubarb Tavern to the dockside pubs with their stories of pirates and smugglers.

0 7524 3475 6

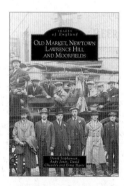

## Old Market, Newtown, Lawrence Hill and Moorfields

DAVID STEPHENSON, ANDY JONES, DAVID CHEESLEY AND ERNIE HASTE

This collection of over 200 old photographs recalls life in Bristol as it was during the last century. Old shops and family businesses are captured, including Angel's Café in Old Market, the Empire Palace of Varieties where many stars, including Gracie Fields and Harry Houdini, walked the boards, and the once-familiar sight of trams.

0 7524 2844 6

If you are interested in purchasing other books published by Tempus, or in case you have difficulty finding any Tempus books in your local bookshop, you can also place orders directly through our website

**www.tempus-publishing.com**